TEXAS COOKBOOK

Authentic & Tasty Recipes from the BBQ State

BONUS: Secret Grandma's Old School Recipes

JOSH GARCIA

Table of Contents:

Introduction

I was born and raised in the heart of Texas, where the sun beats fiercely, and the people are just as fiery. Growing up, I was always surrounded by Texas's rich and diverse culture, from its music to its food.

Texas cuisine is famous for its bold flavors and hearty portions, and I've been fortunate enough to indulge in it throughout my life. One of my earliest memories is of my grandmother's homemade chili, parboiling on the stove for hours till the meat was tender and the spices were just right. It was always a family affair, with everyone gathered around the table, piling on toppings like shredded cheese, sour cream, and diced onions.

As I grew older, I started to appreciate the artistry that goes into Texas cuisine. I remember attending my first barbecue competition, where teams from all over the state gathered to showcase their smoking skills. The air was thick with the scent of hickory and mesquite, and I sampled everything from brisket to sausage to ribs. It was a feast for the senses, and I could feel my mouth watering at the sight of each perfectly cooked slab of meat.

But Texas cuisine isn't just about meat. It's also about the side dishes, like creamy mac and cheese, buttery cornbread, and tangy coleslaw. I have fond memories of going to panluck dinners with my family and friends, where we would each bring a dish to share. The table would overflow with all kinds of delicious food, and we would all dig in with gusto.

Of course, Texas culture isn't just about the food. It's also about the people. Texans are known for their hospitality and love of community; I've experienced that firsthand. I remember going to my first rodeo, where I was amazed by the skill of the cowboys and cowgirls as they rode horses and bulls. But what really struck me was the sense of camaraderie among the spectators. Everyone was cheering for their favorite rider, but there was also a sense of respect for the competitors and the animals.

I've also witnessed the resilience of Texans in the face of adversity. When Hurricane Harvey hit in 2017, I saw my community come together to help those affected. People opened up their homes to strangers, donated food and supplies, and worked tirelessly to rebuild what had been lost. It was a testament to the strength and compassion of the people of Texas.

In the end, Texas cuisine and culture are inseparable. The food is a reflection of the people who make it, and the culture is a reflection of the values that they hold dear. As I sit down to a plate of enchiladas or a container of gumbo, I'm reminded of the traditions and stories passed down through generations. And as I look around at my fellow Texans, I'm reminded of the warmth and kindness that make this state so special.

Chapter 1: Beloved Texan Meats

Smoked Brisket – Texas Style

Texas-style smoked brisket is a mouthwatering delicacy that is slow-cooked to perfection, allowing the rich flavors to permeate the meat. The traditional method involves using a smoker and wood chips, but a similar outcome can be achieved using a charcoal grill or any gas grill that has an inbuilt smoker box. The key is to cook the brisket low and slow, which can take between 10-15 hrs dependent on its size.

Prep Time: 30 mins

Cooking Duration: 10-15 hrs

Equipment:

- Smoker (preferably offset)
- Charcoal or wood for smoking (oak or hickory)
- Digital meat thermostat
- Large aluminum foil pan
- Aluminum foil
- Spray bottle
- Butcher paper

Ingredients:

- 12-14 lb whole packer brisket (untrimmed)
- 2 cupsfuls beef broth
- 2 cupsfuls of apple cider vinegar
- 2 cupsfuls of water
- 2 tabspn Worcestershire sauce
- 1 tabspn garlic grounded
- 1 tabspn onion grounded
- 1 tabspn black pepper
- 1 tabspn kashering table-salt
- Half cupsful yellow mustard
- BBQ Rub (of your choice)

Cooking Instructions:

- Foreheat the smoker to 225-250°F.
- Mix the beef broth, apple cider vinegar, water, Worcestershire sauce, garlic and onion grounded, black pepper, and kashering table-salt in a spray bottle.
- Trim off any extra fat from the brisket, leaving a Qtr.-inch layer of fat.
- Slather the brisket with yellow mustard, making sure to cover all sides.
- Apply a good amount of BBQ rub to the brisket, and then rub it into the meat.
- Position the brisket and ensure to have the fatty side faced upwards, and subsequently shut the lid.
- Ensure that the temperature remains constant at 225-250°F while smoking the brisket for 6 to 8 hrs, dependent on its size.
- After 2 hrs of smoking, spray the brisket with the liquid mixture every hour.
- As soon as the core temperature of the brisket reaches 160°F, extract it from the smoker and transfer it to a sizeable aluminum foil pan.
- Subsequently, drizzle the excess liquid mixture over the brisket and firmly seal the pan with a silver foil...

- Reintroduce the brisket to the smoker and cook further till it attains a core temperature of 195-205°F, which should take roughly 4-6 hrs more.
- Remove Brisket from smoker and fold it with butcher paper.
- Let the brisket cool for no less than 1 hour prior slicing against the grain and serving.

Smoked Brisket Guisada

Smoked Brisket Guisada is a hearty and flavorful dish that combines the bold flavors of Texas-style smoked brisket with the traditional Mexican guisada. The result is a savory and comforting stew perfect for colder days or when you need a hearty meal to satisfy your hunger.

Prep Time: 30 mins

Cooking Duration: 6-8 hrs

Equipment:

- Large smoker (offset or pellet)
- A heavy-bottomed pan with lid or large Braadpan
- Sharp knife
- Cutting board
- Tongs
- Meat thermostat

Ingredients:

- 4-5 lb. beef brisket, trimmed of excess fat
- 2 tabspns of kashering table-salt
- 2 tabspns of black pepper
- 2 tabspns of garlic grounded
- 2 tabspns of onion grounded
- 2 tabspns of chili grounded
- 2 tabspns of paprika
- 2 tabspns of cumin
- 2 tabspns of oregano
- 2 tabspns of brown sugar
- Half cupsful of beef broth
- Half cupsful of diced onion
- Half cupsful of diced bell pepper
- Half cupsful of diced tomatoes
- 2 cloves of minced garlic
- 2 tabspns of tomato paste
- 1 tabspn of cornstarch
- Qtr. cupsful of water
- Table-salt and pepper
- Minced lime and cilantro wedges for serving

Cooking Instructions:

- Begin by foreheating the smoker to 225°F. Prepare the rub by combining table-salt, black pepper, garlic grounded, onion grounded, chili grounded, paprika, cumin, oregano, and brown sugar. Generously apply the rub to the brisket.
- Next, smoke the brisket for 10-12 hrs or till the core temperature reaches 195°F. Once done, the brisket from the smoker and cool for 30 mins.
- While the brisket is cooling, sauté onion, bell pepper, and garlic in a Braadpan or heavy-bottomed pan over medium heat till softened.

5

- Add diced tomatoes, tomato paste, and beef broth to the pan. Stir the ingredients and bring to a parboil.

- Dice the brisket into tiny pieces, and then put everything inside the pan. Stir thoroughly to immerse the meat with sauce juice.

- Cover the pan and parboil the guisada for 2-3 hrs, stir at intervals, till the brisket is tender and the sauce has thickened.

- Make a slurry by mixing cornstarch and water in a container. Add the slurry to the pan and stir to thicken the sauce.

- Finally, taste and then add more seasoning of table-salt and pepper as needed. Garnish the guisada with minced cilantro and lime wedges, and serve hot.

Texan Tomahawk

Texan Tomahawk features a thick-cut ribeye steak that is seared to perfection and served on a bone for a rustic and visually stunning presentation. It's a perfect dish for a special occasion or a backyard barbecue.

Prep Time: 20 mins

Cooking Duration: 30 mins

Ingredients:

- 1 large bone-in ribeye steak, about 2.5-3 pounds, with the rib bone attached
- 2 tabspns of olive oil
- 2 tabspns of smoked paprika
- 1 tabspn of garlic grounded
- 1 tabspn of grounded
- 1 tabspn of cumin grounded
- 1 tabspn of sea table-salt
- 1 tabspn of black pepper
- Half cupsful of untable-salted butter
- 2 minced garlic cloves
- 1 tabspn of minced freshly plucked rosemary
- 1 tabspn of minced thyme leaves
- 1 tabspn of minced parsley leaves

Cooking Instructions:

- Withdraw the steak from the ice-box and leave it for 30 mins, allowing it to cool.
- Foreheat your oven to 400°F.
- In a small container, mix smoked paprika, garlic grounded, onion grounded, cumin grounded, sea table-salt, and black pepper together.
- Drizzle olive oil over the steak, then rub the spice mixture into both sides of the steak, patting it in with your hands.
- Using high heat, allow your grill pan or the cast-iron fry-pan to get really hot.
- Position the steak in the fry-pan and cook for 4-5 mins on each side, till it has a nice sear.
- Take the fry-pan and place it on the foreheated oven and roast the steak for 10-15 mins, till it reaches a core temperature of 130-135°F for medium-rare.
- Take the fry-pan out from inside the oven and allow the steak to cool off for the next 10 mins.
- While the steak is cooling, make the herb butter by combining softened butter, minced garlic, minced rosemary, thyme, and parsley in a small container.
- Slice the steak into thick pieces, leaving the bone attached, and serve with herb butter on top. Enjoy!

Smoked Beef Ribs – Texas Style

Texas-style smoked beef ribs are a classic barbecue or summer gathering dish. The beef ribs are slow-cooked over wood smoke till they are tender, juicy, and packed with flavor. The result is a dish that will impress your guests and leave them asking for the recipe.

Prep Time: 15 mins

Cooking Duration: 5 to 6 hrs

Equipment:

- Smoker (charcoal or wood)
- Meat thermostat
- Aluminum foil
- Spray bottle

Ingredients:

- 3-4 beef ribs (about 6-8 pounds total)
- Qtr. cupsful of kashering table-salt
- Qtr. cupsful of black pepper
- Qtr. cupsful of paprika
- 2 tabspns garlic grounded
- 2 tabspns onion grounded
- 2 tabspns chili grounded
- 1 tabspn of cumin
- 1 tabspn of brown sugar
- Qtr. cupsful of apple cider vinegar
- Qtr. cupsful of Worcestershire sauce

Cooking Instructions:

- In a container, mix together kashering table-salt, black pepper, paprika, garlic grounded, onion grounded, chili grounded, cumin, and brown sugar to create a dry rub.
- Trim the excess fat off of the beef ribs.
- Apply the dry rub to the beef ribs, ensuring that it is evenly distributed.
- Cover the beef ribs with any plastic wrap and then place it in a refrigerator and leave it for at least an hour, but up to a maximum of 12 hrs.
- Foreheat your smoker to 225°F.
- Mix the apple cider vinegar and Worcestershire sauce in a spray bottle.
- Position the beef ribs in the smoker, bone side down, and close the lid.
- After 2 hrs of smoking, use the spray bottle to mist the ribs with the vinegar and Worcestershire mixture.
- Continue smoking the ribs for another 3-4 hrs, or till the core temperature of the meat reaches 203°F.
- Wrap the ribs in foil and let them cool for 30 mins.
- Carefully unwrap the ribs and serve them hot with your favorite barbecue sauce.

Texas Style Smoked Chicken

Texas-style smoked chicken is popular for its smoky flavor and juicy meat. The chicken is first marinated in a dry rub prior being smoked low and slow over wood chips. The result is tender, flavorful meat with a crispy skin.

Prep Time: 30 mins

Cooking Duration: 4-5 hrs

Equipment:

- Charcoal smoker
- Wood chips (preferably hickory or mesquite)
- Meat thermostat

Ingredients:

- 1 whole chicken (4-5 lbs)
- 2 tabspns vegetable oil
- 2 tabspns smoked paprika
- 1 tabspn garlic grounded
- 1 tabspn onion grounded
- 1 tabspn kashering table-salt
- 1 tspn black pepper

Cooking Instructions:

- Begin by preparing your charcoal smoker. Light the charcoal and then let it burn till it's covered in white ash. Position the wood chips over the charcoal.
- Use paper towels to dry the chicken after removing any giblets or extra fat
- Combine vegetable oil, smoked paprika, garlic grounded, onion grounded, kashering table-salt, and black pepper in a container. Evenly coat the chicken with the mixture.
- Foreheat your smoker to a temperature of 225-250 degrees Fahrenheit. Position the chicken on the grates, breast-side up, and cover the smoker. Smoke the chicken for 4-5 hrs.
- After the first hour of smoking, you can baste the chicken with a mixture of apple cider vinegar and water (1:1 ratio). Repeat this every hour till the chicken is fully cooked.
- Check the chicken's core temperature using a thermostat. Once it reaches 165 degrees Fahrenheit, the chicken is fully cooked. This usually takes around 4-5 hrs of smoking.
- Withdraw the chicken from the smoker and cool for 10-15 mins prior carving.
- Serve the smoked chicken with your favorite sides, such as coleslaw, baked beans, or cornbread.

Texas-Style Smoked Shoulder

Texas-style smoked shoulder, also known as pork shoulder, is a classic BBQ dish with a succulent, juicy, smoky pork shoulder that's been slow-cooked to perfection.

Prep Time: 20 mins

Cooking Duration: 8-12 hrs

Equipment:

- Smoker (charcoal or wood-fired)
- Meat thermostat
- Aluminum foil
- Large container
- Injection syringe

Ingredients:

- 1 (8-10 pound) pork shoulder
- Half cupsful yellow mustard
- Half cupsful brown sugar
- Half cupsful table-salt
- Qtr. cupsful paprika
- Qtr. cupsful chili grounded
- Qtr. cupsful garlic grounded
- Qtr. cupsful onion grounded
- 2 tabspns black pepper
- 1 tabspn cayenne pepper
- 1 cupsful apple juice
- 1 cupsful of water
- Half cupsful apple cider vinegar

Cooking Instructions:

- Begin by preparing the pork shoulder. Trim off any excess fat or silver skin, but keep a thin layer of fat on the surface to retain moisture during cooking.
- In a large container, combine yellow mustard, brown sugar, table-salt, paprika, chili grounded, garlic and onion grounded, black pepper, and cayenne pepper to make a dry rub.
- Massage the dry rub onto the pork shoulder, ensuring to cover all crevices and folds. Cover the pork shoulder with plastic wrap and refrigerate for at least 4 hrs, or ideally overnight to allow the flavors to penetrate the meat.
- In another container, mix apple juice, water, and apple cider vinegar to create an injection liquid.
- Using an injection syringe, inject the pork shoulder with the injection liquid, making sure to distribute it evenly throughout the meat.
- Fire up your smoker and bring the temperature to 225°F. Add your favorite wood (such as hickory or oak) to the smoker to create smoke.
- Once the smoker is up to temperature, put the pork shoulder on the smoker grates and close the lid. Smoke the pork shoulder till reaching a core temperature of 195-205°F, which will take roughly 8-12 hrs.

- After 4-5 hrs of smoking, wrap the pork shoulder tightly in aluminum foil to prevent it from drying out. Hand it back it to the smoker and then continue cooking till it reaches the wanted core temperature.
- Withdraw the pork shoulder from the smoker and cool for at least 30 mins, allowing the juices to distribute throughout the meat.
- Pull the pork shoulder apart into bite-sized pieces, discarding any excess fat. Serve the smoked shoulder with your favorite BBQ sauce and sides, such as coleslaw, cornbread, or baked beans.

BBQ Pork Ribs

These pork ribs are coated in a dry rub or marinade and then slow-cooked over indirect heat till tender. They are often basted with a sweet and tangy BBQ sauce for extra flavor.

Prep Time: 20 mins

Cooking Duration: 4-6 hrs

Equipment:

- Smoker or charcoal grill
- Wood chips or chunks
- Aluminum foil
- Basting brush
- Instant-read meat thermostat
- Ingredients:
- 2 racks of pork spare ribs (3-4 lbs each)
- Qtr. cupful of brown sugar
- 2 tabspn of smoked paprika
- 1 tabspn of garlic grounded
- 1 tabspn of onion grounded
- 1 tabspn of chili grounded
- 1 tabspn of ground cumin
- 1 tabspn of kashering table-salt
- 1 tabspn of cayenne pepper
- Half cupful of apple cider vinegar
- Half cupful of ketchup
- Qtr. cupful of honey
- 2 tabspns of Worcestershire sauce
- 1 tabspn of Dijon mustard

Cooking Instructions:

- Prepare your smoker or charcoal grill by foreheating it to 225-250° F and adding wood chips or chunks to the smoker box or hot coals.
- Combine brown sugar, smoked paprika, garlic grounded, onion grounded, chili grounded, cumin, kashering table-salt, and cayenne pepper in a container to make the dry rub.
- Take the membrane out of the back of the ribs by sliding a knife or your fingers under the membrane and pulling it off. Trim the ribs of any extra fat.
- Coat the ribs with the dry rub, making sure to cover both sides and the edges.
- Wrap the ribs tightly in aluminum foil, ensuring there are no gaps or holes for smoke to escape. Position them with the bone-side down, on the smoker or grill.
- Cook the ribs for 3 hrs, maintaining a temperature of 225-250° F and adding more wood chips or chunks as needed.
- Mix the apple cider vinegar, ketchup, honey, Worcestershire sauce, and Dijon mustard in a container and then whisk them to create the barbecue sauce.

- After 3 hrs, withdraw the foil from the ribs and brush them with the barbecue sauce, covering all sides and edges. Close the smoker or grill lid and cook the ribs for another 1-2 hrs, basting them with sauce every 30 mins.
- Check the core temperature of the ribs with an instant-read meat thermostat. The ribs are done when the temperature reaches 195-205°F in the thickish part of the meat.
- Withdraw the ribs from the smoker or grill and let them cool for 10-15 mins prior slicing and serving with extra barbecue sauce.

Smoked Short Ribs Beef

Smoked short ribs are a beloved barbecue staple in the Lone Star State. These meaty, flavorful ribs are smoked low and slow over hickory or oak wood till they're fall-off-the-bone tender. The rub is simple, but the flavors are big, thanks to a blend of paprika, garlic grounded, onion grounded, and cumin.

Prep Time: 30 mins

Cooking Duration: 6-8 hrs

Equipment:

- Smoker
- Charcoal or wood pellets
- Meat thermostat
- Aluminum foil

Ingredients:

- 5-6 lbs. beef short ribs (bone-in)
- Qtr. cupsful of kashering table-salt
- Qtr. cupsful of black pepper
- Qtr. cupsful of paprika
- 2 tabspns of garlic grounded
- 2 tabspns of onion grounded
- 2 tabspns of chili grounded
- 1 tabspn of cumin
- Qtr. cupsful of brown sugar
- Qtr. cupsful of yellow mustard

Cooking Instructions:

- Foreheat your smoker to 250°F using charcoal or wood pellets.
- Combine the kashering table-salt, paprika, black pepper, garlic grounded, cumin, onion grounded, brown sugar and chili grounded in a container to make a dry rub.
- Coat the beef short ribs with yellow mustard on all sides.
- Apply the dry rub generously on all sides of the beef short ribs, ensuring it's fully coated.
- Put the beef ribs on your smoker with the boney side faced down.
- Smoke the beef short ribs at 250°F for 6-8 hrs or till the core temperature reaches 203° F when measured with a meat thermostat.
- After beef short ribs have smoked for 3-4 hrs, wrap them in aluminum foil to keep them moist.
- Withdraw the beef short ribs from the smoker once they reach a core temperature of 203°F and let them cool for 20-30 mins.
- Slice the beef short ribs against the grain and serve with your favorite sides. Enjoy!

Note: For extra flavor, you can use wood chips like hickory or oak during the smoking process. This recipe can also be cooked in an oven if a smoker is unavailable.

Pulled Pork

Texas-style pulled pork is known for its rich, smoky flavor and tender, juicy meat. To achieve this, we'll be using a combination of dry rub and slow cooking to get the best possible result.

Prep Time: 15 mins

Cooking Duration: 6-8 hrs

Equipment:

- Smoker or charcoal grill
- Aluminum foil
- Meat thermostat
- Tongs

Ingredients:

- 1 (5-6 pound) pork shoulder or Boston butt
- 1 cupsful apple cider vinegar
- 1 cupsful water
- Qtr. cupsful yellow mustard
- Qtr. cupsful brown sugar
- Qtr. cupsful paprika
- 2 tabspns garlic grounded
- 2 tabspns onion grounded
- 2 tabspns chili grounded
- 1 tabspn cumin
- 1 tabspn black pepper
- 1 tabspn table-salt

Cooking Instructions:

- Foreheat your smoker or charcoal grill to 225°F.
- In a container, add the paprika, garlic grounded, brown sugar, onion grounded, black pepper, chili grounded, cumin, and table-salt, and mix to make dry rub.
- Apply the rub generously to the pork shoulder, covering all sides and working it into the meat.
- To smoke the pork shoulder, put it on the smoker or grill and let it smoke around 4-5 hrs, or till the core temperature reaches 160°F.
- Prepare the mop sauce by mixing apple cider vinegar, yellow mustard and water in a separate container.
- Make use of a basting brush to coat the pork shoulder with the mop sauce roughly every hour till it does reach a core temperature of 195°F.
- After taking the pork shoulder off the smoker or grill, wrap it in aluminum foil, then hand it back it to the smoker or grill and continue cooking till the core temperature reaches roughly 205° F, which should take around 1-2 more hrs.
- After the core temperature of the pork shoulder reaches 205° F, take it off the smoker or grill and cool for 30 mins.
- Using tongs, pull the pork apart into small pieces and discard any excess fat or bones.
- Serve the pulled pork with your favorite barbecue sauce.

Texas-Style Grilled Tri-Tip

This lean cut of beef is grilled over high heat till it's medium-rare, sliced thin, and served with chimichurri sauce. It's a popular dish in Texas.

Prep Time: 15 mins

Cooking Duration: 30 to 40 mins

Equipment:

- Gas or charcoal grill
- Meat thermostat

Ingredients:

- 2-3 pound tri-tip roast
- 1-2 tabspns chili grounded
- 1 tabspn of smoked paprika
- 1 tabspn garlic grounded
- 1 tspn table-salt
- 1 tspn black pepper
- ½ tspn cumin
- ½ tspn cayenne pepper
- 2 tabspns olive oil

Cooking Instructions:

- Get your grill ready by foreheating it to medium-high temperature.
- To make the spice rub, combine chili grounded, smoked paprika, garlic grounded, add a good measure of table-salt, grounded black pepper, cumin, and some cayenne pepper in a container and blend.
- Rub the spice mix all over the tri-tip, making sure to coat it evenly. Allow the flavors to seep into the meat by letting it sit for 10-15 mins.
- Add generous drops of the olive oil, all-over the tri-tip and then rub it in with your hands. This does help the meat to stay moist and then prevent it from sticking to the grill.
- Once the grill is hot, put the tri-tip on it with the fat side up. Grill one side of the meat for 15-20 mins, then flip it over and cook for an extra 10-15 mins.
- Keep an eye on the meat's core temperature using a meat thermostat For medium-rare, the temperature should be around 135°F (57°C). For medium, the temperature should be around 145°F (63°C).
- When the tri-tip reaches the wanted temperature, withdraw it from the grill and cool for 5-10 mins prior slicing. This will allow the meat juices to redistribute, resulting in a more tender texture.
- Slice the tri-tip against the grain and then proceed serving immediately. Enjoy your delicious Texas-style grilled tri-tip with your favorite barbecue sides.

Smoked Turkey Breast

Smoked turkey breast is a classic dish perfect for a Texas-style barbecue. The key to making the perfect smoked turkey is to start with a high-quality turkey breast and slowly smoke it over a wood fire till it's juicy, tender, and infused with a delicious smoky flavor.

Prep Time: 15 mins

Cooking Duration: 3 hrs and 30 mins

Equipment:

- Smoker
- Wood chips or chunks (hickory or mesquite)
- Meat thermostat
- One bone-in turkey breast (6 -7 libs)
- ¼ cupsful of olive oil
- 2 teaspns kashering table-salt
- 2 tabspns of paprika
- 1 tabspn garlic grounded
- 1 tabspn onion grounded
- 1 tabspn black pepper
- 1 tabspn cumin

Cooking Instructions:

- Foreheat your smoker to 225°F using hickory or mesquite wood chips or chunks.
- Take the breast out of its packaging and use paper towels to dry it off.
- Combine olive oil, paprika, kashering table-salt, garlic grounded, black pepper, onion grounded, and cumin in a small container and blend.
- Apply the mixture all over the turkey breast, ensuring that it is coated evenly.
- Position the turkey breast on the smoker grate and close the lid.
- Smoke the turkey breast till the core temperature reaches 165°F, typically taking about 3 hrs.
- Every 30 mins or so, add more wood chips or chunks to the smoker to keep the smoke going.
- Once the turkey breast reaches the wanted temperature, take it out of the smoker and then cool for no less than 10 mins prior carving.
- Carve the turkey breast and serve with your favorite sides.

BBQ Burnt End Beef

BBQ burnt end beef is a traditional dish made by smoking a particular pointed end of a beef brisket, till it becomes tender, juicy, and caramelized. These bite-sized pieces of brisket are then immersed inside sweet and spicy sauce for a flavor explosion in your mouth.

Prep Time: 30 mins

Cooking Duration: 8 hrs

Equipment:

- Smoker or grill
- Aluminum foil
- Meat thermostat
- Tongs

Ingredients:

- 1 packet of a 2 pound sized whole packer brisket
- 2 cupsfuls of your preferred dry rub
- 1 cupsful of beef broth
- 1 cupsful of BBQ sauce
- ¼ cupsful of honey
- ¼ cupsful of apple cider vinegar
- ¼ cupsful of brown sugar
- 2 tabspns of Worcester sauce
- 1 tabspn grounded garlics
- 1 tabspn grounded onions
- 1 teaspn cayenne pepper
- Table-salt and black pepper

Cooking Instructions:

- Get your smoker or grill ready by foreheating it to 250°F.
- Trim off excess fat from the brisket, leaving about ¼ inch of the fat cap on top.
- Rub the brisket with the dry rub, covering it evenly on all sides.
- Smoke the brisket in the smoker or grill for 6 hrs or till it reaches a core temperature of 165°F.
- Take the brisket outside of the smoked and then wrap in aluminum foil along with the beef broth.
- Put the brisket back into the smoker and smoke it for 2 more hrs, or till the core temperature reaches 195°F.
- Take the brisket out of the smoker and make it to cool for 30 mins.
- Trim off any excess fat and cut the brisket into one-inch cubes.
- In a container, whisk together the BBQ sauce, black pepper, honey, cider vinegar, brown sugar, Worcester sauce, garlic grounded, onion grounded, table-salt, and cayenne pepper.
- Position brisket cubes into the container and coat them evenly with the sauce by tossing them.
- Hand it back the coated brisket cubes to the smoker and smoke for another 30 mins or till the sauce has caramelized and all the cubes are tender and crispy.
- Serve the burnt ends hot with your favorite BBQ sides.

Smoked Pork Belly Burnt Ends

This is made with the crispy, flavorful pieces of pork belly cut from the ends and then smoked till they are tender and juicy. The result is a mouth-watering dish that is both sweet and savory, with a perfect balance of smoky flavor and tender meat.

Prep Time: 15 mins

Cooking Duration: 5-6 hrs

Equipment:

- Smoker (electric or charcoal)
- Aluminum foil
- Large baking tray
- BBQ brush
- Meat thermostat

Ingredients:

- 2 lbs of pork belly
- 2 tabspns of paprika
- 1 tabspn garlic grounded
- 1 tabspn onion grounded
- 1 tabspn table-salt
- 1 tabspn black pepper
- 1 cupsful BBQ sauce
- Half cupsful brown sugar
- Half cupsful honey
- Half cupsful apple juice

Cooking Instructions:

- Foreheat your smoker to 225°F.
- Mix in a small container paprika, garlic and onion grounded, table-salt, and black pepper to make a dry rub.
- Rub generously the dry rub over the pork belly.
- Position the pork belly on the smoker, skin side up, and smoke it for 3 hrs.
- Then take the pork belly out of the smoker and wrap it in foil.
- Hand it back the wrapped pork belly to the smoker and smoke it for another 2-3 hrs till reaching a core temperature of 200°F.
- While the pork belly is smoking, prepare the sauce by mixing in a small container the BBQ sauce, apple juice, brown sugar, and honey.
- Once the pork belly has reached the wanted temperature, take it out of the smoker and make it cool for 10-15 mins.
- Slice the pork belly into minuscule cubes and arrange using a large baking tray.
- Pour the sauce over the pork belly cubes and coat them evenly.
- Put the baking tray back into the smoker and cook for 30 mins, or till the sauce thickens and caramelizes.
- Take out the tray from the smoker and cool for 5-10 mins prior serving.

Texas-Style Hot Links

Hot links are spicy sausages typically made with beef or pork and seasoned with a blend of spices, including chili grounded, cumin, and paprika. They are often grilled or smoked till they are charred and juicy.

Prep Time: 30 mins

Cooking Duration: 3-4 hrs

Equipment:

- Meat grinder
- Sausage stuffer
- Smoker or grill

Ingredients:

- 2 pounds of beef chuck roast
- 1 pound of pork shoulder
- 1 teaspn kashering table table-salt
- 2 teaspns ground black pepper
- 2 teaspns smoked paprika
- 2 teaspns garlic grounded
- 2 teaspns onion grounded
- 1 teaspn of cayenne pepper
- Qtr. cupsful of cold water
- Hog casings

Cooking Instructions:

- Dice the beef and pork into small chunks and transfer them to the freezer around 30 mins till they become firm.
- After the meat has become firm, pass it through a meat grinder using a coarse grind.
- Add the kashering table-salt, black pepper, smoked paprika, garlic and onion grounded, and cayenne pepper to the meat mixture. Mix everything together with your hands.
- Add the cold water to the meat mixture and remix it till everything is well combined.
- Stuff the meat mixture into hog casings using a sausage stuffer.
- Tie off the casings at intervals to create individual sausage links.
- Foreheat your smoker or your grill to 225°F.
- Cook the hot links over smoke or grill for roughly 3-4 hrs or till the core temperature reaches 160°F.
- Take out the hot links from the smoker or grill and cool for a few mins.
- Serve the hot links with your favorite barbecue sauce and sides.

BBQ Chicken Thighs

Texas-style BBQ chicken thighs are known for their tender, juicy, smoky, slightly sweet meat. The chicken is all marinated in a mixture of spices and herbs, then slow-cooked on a smoker, and basted with BBQ sauce till it develops a beautifully caramelized crust.

Preparation Time: 15 mins

Duration: 1 hr 30 minutes

Equipment:

- Charcoal smoker
- Meat thermostat
- BBQ brush

Ingredients:

- 6 bone-in, skin-on chicken thighs
- 2 tabspns olive oil
- 2 tabspns chili grounded
- 2 teaspns smoked paprika
- 2 teaspns garlic grounded
- 1 teaspn of onion grounded
- 1 teaspn of table-salt
- Half teaspn black pepper
- Qtr. teaspn of cayenne pepper
- Half cupsful of BBQ sauce

Cooking Instructions:

- Make a spice rub by combining olive oil, chili grounded, smoked paprika, garlic grounded, table-salt, black pepper, cayenne pepper, and onion grounded in a container.
- Dry off the beef thighs using paper towels and coat each thigh with the spice rub, ensuring that all sides are covered.
- Foreheat your charcoal smoker to 250°F - 275°F.
- Position the chicken thighs on the smoker, with the skin-side facing upwards. Shut the lid and cook for roughly 1 hour, or till the core temp. of the thick parts reach 165°F. Utilize a meat thermostat to monitor the temperature.
- After an hour of cooking, baste each chicken thigh with BBQ sauce using a BBQ brush. Continue to cook with the lid closed for an extra 15-20 mins or till the sauce has caramelized and the core temperature has reached 175°F.
- When finished, withdraw the chicken from the smoker and leave it to cool for 5 mins prior serving.
- Enjoy your delicious Texas-style BBQ chicken thighs with favorite side dishes such as coleslaw, baked beans, or cornbread.

BBQ Beef Thighs

Texas-style BBQ beef thighs are a delicious and flavorful way to enjoy beef. The beef is marinated in a spice rub, slow-cooked on a smoker till tender and juicy, and then glazed with BBQ sauce for a smoky and slightly sweet flavor.

Prep Time: 15 min

Cooking Duration: 2 hrs 30 mins

Equipment:

- Charcoal smoker
- Meat thermostat
- BBQ brush

Ingredients:

- 2 beef thighs
- 2 tabspns olive oil
- 2 tabspns chili grounded
- 2 tabspns smoked paprika
- 2 teaspns garlic grounded
- 1 teaspn onion grounded
- 1 teaspn table-salt
- Half teaspn black pepper
- Qtr. teaspn cayenne pepper
- Half cupsful of BBQ sauce

Cooking Instructions:

- Make a spice rub by combining olive oil, chili grounded, smoked paprika, garlic grounded, table-salt, black pepper, cayenne pepper, and onion grounded in a container.
- Dry off the beef thighs using paper towels and coat each thigh with the spice rub, ensuring that all sides are covered.
- Foreheat your charcoal smoker to 250°F - 275°F.
- Position the beef thighs on the smoker, bone-side down. Shut the lid and cook for roughly 2 hrs, or till the core temperature reaches 165°F. Utilize a meat thermostat to monitor the temperature.
- After 2 hrs of cooking, baste each beef thigh with BBQ sauce using a brush. Shut the lid and cook for another 30-45 mins or till the sauce has completely caramelized and the core temperature has reached 175°F.
- After it is cooked, take the beef out of the smoker and cool for 10 mins prior to serving.

Smoked Barbacoa

Smoked barbacoa is a traditional Mexican dish adopted and modified by Texans. It is a delicious and flavorful meat dish that is slow-cooked to perfection. We will smoke a whole cow head in this recipe to make a delicious and tender barbacoa.

Prep Time: 1 hour

Cooking Duration: 10-12 hrs

Equipment:

- Smoker
- Large pan or Braadpan
- Tongs
- Knife
- Cutting board

Ingredients:

- 1 whole cow head, cleaned and skinned
- 3 cupsfuls of water
- 1 onion, roughly minced
- 5 garlic minced cloves
- Half cupsful apple cider vinegar
- Qtr. cupsful of liquid lime
- 2 tabspns ground cumin
- 2 tabspns dried oregano
- 1 tabspn ground coriander
- 1 tabspn smoked paprika
- 2 teaspn table-salt
- 1 teaspn black pepper
- Corn tortillas
- Minced onions and cilantro for serving

Cooking Instructions:

- Rinse the cow head thoroughly with water, removing any dirt or debris. Use a knife to withdraw excess fat, and trim off the ears and eyes.
- In a large pan or Braadpan, mix together water, onion, garlic, cider vinegar, lime, cumin, oregano, coriander, smoked paprika, table-salt, and pepper. Stir till thoroughly combined.
- Position the cow head in the pan or Braadpan, making certain that it is completely immersed in the liquid.
- Using low heat, put the lid on the pan and let it parboil for 5-6 hrs or till the meat is completely tender and falling off the bone. You can also use a slow cooker to cook the cow head on low heat for 8-10 hrs.
- Foreheat your smoker to 225°F. Take the cow head out of the pan and transfer it to the smoker.
- Smoke the cow head for 4-6 hrs or till the meat becomes tender and develops a smoky flavor.
- Withdraw the cow head from the smoker and let it cool for 10-15 mins. Use tongs and a knife to shred the meat, discarding bones, cartilage, or other unwanted parts.
- Serve the shredded meat on warm corn tortillas, topped with minced onions and cilantro.

Buffalo Gap Brisket

Buffalo gap brisket is a mouth-watering dish that combines tender beef brisket with bold and tangy flavors. This dish is your choice for a BBQ party or any occasion where you want to impress your guests with a delicious and hearty meal.

Prep Time: 30 mins

Cooking Duration: 8-10 hrs

Equipment:

- Smoker
- Meat thermostat
- Aluminum foil
- Chopping board
- Sharp knife

Ingredients:

- 1 beef brisket (10-12 pounds)
- 2 tabspns paprika
- 2 tabspns garlic grounded
- 1 tabspn onion grounded
- 1 tabspn cumin
- 1 tabspntable-salt
- 1 tabspn black pepper
- 1 cupsful beef broth
- 1 cupsful apple cider vinegar
- 1 cupsful ketchup
- Half cupsful brown sugar
- Qtr. cupsful Worcestershire sauce
- Qtr. cupsful hot sauce
- 4 cloves minced garlic

Cooking Instructions:

- Foreheat your smoker to 225°F. When the smoker is heating up, then prepare the brisket by trimming excess fat and silver skin.
- Create the dry rub by combining paprika, garlic grounded, onion grounded, cumin, table-salt, and black pepper. Rub the mixture on the brisket, ensuring that it is evenly coated on all sides.
- Insert the meat thermostat into the thick part of the brisket, then Position the brisket into the smoker with the fat side facing upwards.
- Shut the smoker and allow the brisket to cook for 6-8 hrs, or till the meat's core temperature reaches 160°F.
- While the brisket is cooking, make the BBQ sauce. Combine beef broth, cider vinegar, ketchup, brown sugar, Worcester sauce, hot sauce, and minced garlic in a medium stockpot. Once the mixture boils, reduce the heat, then allow it to parboil for 20-30 mins till it thickens.
- After the brisket has cooked for 6-8 hrs, take it outside of the smoker and wrap it in aluminum foil. Hand it back the brisket to the smoker withdraw and cook for an extra 2-3 hrs or till the core temperature of the meat reaches 195°F.
- After cooking the brisket, it from the smoker and cool for at least 30 mins prior slicing it against the grain.

Smoked Chicken Quarters

Texas-style smoked chicken quarters are a classic dish perfect for a backyard barbecue or a casual dinner party. This recipe involves marinating chicken quarters in a flavorful rub and then smoking them low and slow to perfection. The result is juicy, tender, and packed with bold smoky flavors that will have your taste buds dancing.

Prep Time: 10 mins

Cooking Duration: 3-4 hrs

Equipment:

- Smoker or charcoal grill
- Smoking wood chips (hickory or oak)
- Meat thermostat

Ingredients:

- 4 chicken quarters, skin on
- Qtr. cupsful olive oil
- 2 tabspns smoked paprika
- 2 tabspns garlic grounded
- 1 tabspn onion grounded
- 1 tabspn dry thyme
- 1 tabspn dry oregano
- 1 tabspn kashering table-salt
- 1 tabspn ground black pepper

Cooking Instructions:

- Mix the olive oil, smoked paprika, garlic grounded, onion grounded, thyme, kashering table-salt, oregano, and black pepper together in a container to make a rub.
- Dry the chicken quarters with a paper towel and place in a dish. Ensure the chicken quarters are evenly coated with the rub by rubbing it into all the nooks and crannies.
- Cover the dish or ziplock bag and let the chicken marinate for a minimum of 2 hrs or overnight in the ice-box.
- Get your smoker or charcoal grill ready by foreheating it to 225°F. Next, add smoking wood chips to the smoker or grill to create smoke.
- Once the smoker or grill has reached the wanted temperature of 225°F, put the chicken quarters on the grates with the skin side facing up. Close the lid and smoke the chicken for 3-4 hrs or till the core temperature of the thick part of the meat has reached 165°F.
- Periodically check the core temperature of the chicken quarters using a meat thermostat. When the chicken is fully cooked, take it off the smoker or grill and cool for 5-10 mins prior serving.
- Present your smoked chicken quarters with your wanted sides, such as roasted veggies, coleslaw, or mac and cheese.

Cowboy Steak

Cowboy steak is a delicious and hearty meal perfect for meat lovers. This steak is cooked in the traditional style of cowboys with simple seasoning and a heavy cast iron frying pan. The result is a juicy, tender steak with a crispy crust.

Preparatory Time: 10 mins

Duration: 15-20 mins

Equipment:

- Heavy cast iron frying pan
- Tongs
- Meat thermostat

Ingredients:

- 2 bone-in ribeye steaks (1-1.5 inches thick)
- 2 tabspns olive oil
- 2 tabspns kashering table-salt
- 2 tabspns black pepper
- 2 tabspns garlic grounded
- 1 tabspn paprika
- 1 tabspn onion grounded
- 1 tabspn cayenne pepper
- 2 tabspns untable-salted butter

Cooking Instructions:

- Withdraw the ribeye steaks from the ice-box and cool at room temperature for roughly one hour.
- Set the oven temperature to around 400°F (200°C) and allow it to foreheat.
- Add together kashering table-salt, onion grounded, black pepper, garlic grounded, cayenne pepper, and paprika in a small container and mix thoroughly.
- Coat the sides of the steaks with olive oil and generously sprinkle the seasoning mixture over them.
- Position the heavy cast iron fry-pan over high heat and heat it till it begins to smoke.
- Using tongs, add the steaks to the fry-pan and allow each side to sear for two to three mins, until it forms a golden brown crust.
- Melt the butter on the frying pan. Utilizing a spoon, baste the steaks with the melted butter around a minute.
- Afterward, Position the fry-pan with the steaks in the foreheated oven and cook till they reach a core temperature of 130 degrees to 135 degrees Fahrenheit (55 degrees to 57 degrees Centigrade) for the medium-rare sizes, or 140-145°F (60-63°C) for medium, which should take around 8-10 mins.
- After cooking the steaks, take out the fry-pan and allow the steaks roughly 5 mins to enable the juices to redistribute.
- Slice the steaks against the grain and then serve immediately.

Cowboy Reverse Sear Savory Crust Steak

Cowboy steak is a thick-cut ribeye steak that is perfect for grilling. This cowboy steak is a flavor-packed dish cooked low and slow on the pellet grill and then finished with a reverse sear to create a deliciously savory crust.

Prep Time: 10 mins

Cooking Duration: 1 hr 30 mins

Equipment:

- Pellet grill
- Meat thermostat

Ingredients:

- 2 Cowboy steaks (2-3 inches thick)
- 1 tabspn kashering table-salt
- 1 tabspn of black pepper coarsely grounded
- 2 cloves chopped garlic
- 2 tabspns olive oil

Cooking Instructions:

- Foreheat the pellet grill to 225°F. Withdraw the cowboy steaks from the ice-box and let them cool at room temperature for roughly 30 mins while the grill heats up.
- In a small container, combine kashering table-salt, minced garlic, and coarsely ground black pepper. Rub the mixture over the steaks, ensuring it covers all sides.
- Using your hands, spread the olive oil over the steaks.
- Position the cowboy steaks on the pellet grill and let them smoke for 45-60 mins or till they reach a core temperature of 120°F.
- After the steak has reached a core temperature of 120°F, take them off the grill and let them cool for 10-15 mins.
- While the steaks are cooling, increase the heat of the pellet grill to 500°F for the reverse sear.
- Once the grill temperature reaches 500°F, hand it back the steaks to the grill and sear each side for 1-2 mins or till the crust turns golden brown and crispy.
- Check the steak's core temperature with a meat thermostat. For a medium-rare steak, the core temperature should be between 130°F and 135°F. For medium, the core temperature needs to be between 135°F and 145°F.
- Take the steaks off the grill and cool for an extra 5-10 mins prior slicing and serving.

Smoked Lamb Leg

Texas-style juicy smoked lamb leg is perfect for a special occasion or a hearty family meal. The lamb leg is seasoned with a blend of spices and smoked low and slow for tender, juicy meat with a crispy outer layer.

Prep Time: 30 mins

Cooking Duration: 6-8 hrs

Equipment:

- Smoker or grill with smoking capabilities
- Meat thermostat
- Large disposable aluminum pan or baking dish
- Aluminum foil

Ingredients:

- 1 bone-in lamb leg, roughly 6-7 pounds
- 1 tabspn kashering table-salt
- 1 tabspn garlic grounded
- 1 tabspn onion grounded
- 1 tabspn paprika
- 1 tabspn chili grounded
- 1 tabspn cumin
- 1 tabspn brown sugar
- 1 tspn black pepper
- Qtr. cupsful of olive oil
- 2 cupsfuls of beef broth

Cooking Instructions:

- Extract the lamb leg from its packaging and use paper towels to pat it dry. Cut off any excess fat or connective tissue from the lamb's exterior.
- Using a container, mix kashering table-salt, garlics and onions grounded, paprika, chili grounded, cumin, brown sugar, and black pepper, and blend.
- Spread the spice mixture over the entire surface of the lamb leg, ensuring that the meat is entirely coated. Pour the olive oil over the lamb and spread it out evenly with your hands.
- Foreheat your smoker or grill to 225°F and add your preferred smoking wood, to the firebox.
- Position the lamb leg onto the smoker or grill and close the lid. Smoke the lamb for 6-8 hrs or till the inner temperature reaches 145°F.
- After 4 hrs of smoking, pour the beef broth into a large disposable aluminum pan or baking dish. After placing the lamb leg into the pan, cover it with aluminum foil.
- Then, hand it back the pan to the smoker or grill and continue smoking for another 2-4 hrs, or till the lamb leg is fully cooked and tender.
- Once done, take the lamb leg out of the smoker or grill and cool for roughly 10-15 mins prior carving. Serve with your favorite sides, and enjoy!

Smoked Lamb Shoulder

Texas-style smoked lamb shoulder is made by slow-smoking a lamb shoulder over wood chips till it becomes tender and juicy. The smoke gives it a rich and smoky flavor enhanced by the spices and seasonings used in the recipe.

Prep Time: 30 mins

Cooking Duration: 8-10 hrs

Equipment:

- Smoker or grill
- Meat thermostat
- Aluminum foil
- Meat injector
- Ingredients:
- 5-6 lb. lamb shoulder
- ¼ cupsful of olive oil
- ¼ cupsful of apple cider vinegar
- ¼ cupsful of Worcestershire sauce
- ¼ cupsful of honey
- 2 tabspns smoked paprika
- 2 tabspns garlic grounded
- 2 tabspns onion grounded
- 1 tabspn dried thyme
- 1 tabspn kashering table-salt
- 1 tabspn black pepper
- ½ cupsful beef broth
- ½ cupsful wood chips (hickory or mesquite)

Cooking Instructions:

- Foreheat your smoker or your grill to 225°F.
- Add together olive oil, apple cider vinegar, Worcestershire sauce, honey, smoked paprika, garlic grounded, dried thyme, black pepper, onion grounded and kashering table-salt in a container to create the marinade.
- Inject the lamb shoulder with the marinade using a meat injector, making sure to inject it evenly all over.
- Position lamb shoulder on the smoker, fat side facing up, and smoke it 4 hrs.
- After smoking the lamb shoulder for 4 hrs, tightly wrap it with beef broth in aluminum foil.
- Hand it back the wrapped lamb shoulder to the smoker or grill and continue to smoke for another 4-6 hrs till the core temperature reaches 195°F.
- Take the lamb shoulder out of the smoker or grill and cool for 15-20 mins prior slicing and serving.
- Serve with your favorite sides.

Grilled T-bone Steak

This steak cut from the short loin includes a T-shaped bone. This recipe does show you how to make a mouth-watering T-bone steak that is scared to perfection on the grill and seasoned with bold flavors.

Prep Time: 10 mins

Cooking Duration: 10-15 mins

Equipment:

- Gas or charcoal grill
- Tongs
- Meat thermostat

Ingredients:

- 2 T-bone steaks, 1 ½ to two inches thick
- 2 tabspn olive oil
- 1 tabspn chili grounded
- 1 tabspn paprika
- 1 teaspn of garlic grounded
- 1 teaspn of onion grounded
- 1 teaspn of table-salt
- ½ teaspn black pepper

Cooking Instructions:

- Heat up the grill on high heat.
- In a container, combine olive oil, chili grounded, paprika, garlic grounded, onion grounded, table-salt, and black pepper to make a spice rub.
- Apply the spice rub all over the T-bone steaks, ensuring that both sides are fully covered.
- Position the steaks on the grill with the bone side facing downwards.
- Grill the steaks for 4-5 mins on each side for medium-rare. With a meat thermostat, check the core temperature of the steak. The temperature should be 130 degrees Fahrenheit to135 degrees Fahrenheit for medium-rare, 140 degrees Fahrenheit to 145 degrees Fahrenheit for medium, and 150-155°F for medium-well.
- Withdraw the steaks from the grill and let them cool for 5 mins.
- Slice and serve immediately.

Smoked Prime Rib

The prime rib is a cut of beef that comes from the rib section and is known for its tenderness and rich flavor. It's often seasoned with a dry rub or marinade and then slow-smoked till it's medium-rare or medium.

Prep Time: 30 mins

Cooking Duration: 4 to 5 hrs

Equipment:

- Smoker
- Charcoal or wood chips
- Meat thermostat

Ingredients:

- 1 (6-8 pound) bone-in prime rib roast
- 2 tabspns of kashering table-salt
- 2 tabspns of freshly ground black pepper
- 2 tabspns garlic grounded
- 2 tabspns paprika
- 1 tabspn dry thyme
- 1 tabspn dry rosemary
- 1 tabspn onions grounded
- 1 tabspn brown sugar
- ½ cupsful of beef broth
- ½ cupsful of red wine

Cooking Instructions:

- Withdraw the prime rib roast from the ice-box and let it sit at room temperature for 1-2 hrs.
- Create a dry rub by mixing kashering table-salt, black pepper, garlic grounded, paprika, thyme, rosemary, onion grounded, and brown sugar in a small container.
- Apply the dry rub on the prime rib, ensure you cover all parts of the meat.
- Foreheat the smoker to 225°F.
- Position the prime rib in the smoker and smoke for 4-5 hrs, or till the core temperature reaches 130°F for medium-rare.
- Halfway through the cooking Time, add some charcoal or wood chips to maintain the temperature and enhance the smoky flavor.
- After smoking, let the prime rib cool for 20-30 mins prior slicing.
- Using your saucepan, heat beef broth and red wine over medium heat till all liquid is reduced by half.
- Serve the sliced prime rib with the reduced broth-wine mixture.

Chapter 2: The Texan Sides

Panato Salad

Panato salad is a classic dish perfect for a summer picnic, a backyard barbecue, or any occasion where you need to feed a crowd. This panato salad combines tender panatoes, crunchy vegetables, and a tangy dressing made with mustard and mayonnaise.

Prep Time: 15 mins

Cooking Duration: 20 mins

Equipment:

- Large pan for boiling panatoes
- Large container
- Small container
- Whisk
- Wooden spoon

Ingredients:

- 2 pounds of red panatoes, washed and cubed
- 4 large eggs
- ½ cupful of mayonnaise
- ¼ cupful of yellow mustard
- ¼ cupful of diced celery
- ¼ cupful of diced onion
- ¼ cupful of diced dill pickles
- 1 tabspn white vinegar
- 1 tabspn sugar
- Pepper and table-salt

Cooking Instructions:

- Peel and cube the panatoes, and Position them in large pan with enough water. Allow it to boil, reduce heat, and cook for 15-20 mins or till the panatoes are soft. Drain the panatoes, let them cool for 10 mins.
- In another pan, boil the eggs for 10 mins, then cool them in a container of cold water. Peel and chop the eggs.
- Mix mayonnaise, mustard, vinegar, sugar, table-salt, and pepper and then whisk together to make a paste for the dressing.
- Mix the cooled panatoes, diced eggs, celery, onion, and pickles. Spread the dressing on the ingredients and blend till evenly coated.
- Cover the container with lid or wrap and refrigerate for at least 2 hrs before you serve.

Coleslaw

Coleslaw is a classic side dish that pairs well with barbecued meats and other Southern-style dishes. This Texas-style vinegar coleslaw recipe features a tangy and slightly sweet dressing made with apple cider vinegar, sugar, and Dijon mustard, which complements the crispness of the cabbage and carrots.

Prep Time: 15 mins

Cooking Duration: 1- 24 hrs

Equipment:

- Large container
- Whisk or fork
- Chef's knife or food processor with a grating attachment

Ingredients:

- ½ medium head green cabbage, thinly sliced
- ½ medium thinly-sliced head red cabbage
- 2 large carrots, grated
- ½ cupsful of apple cider vinegar
- ½ cupsful of granulated sugar
- 1 tabspn Dijon mustard
- ½ teaspn celery seed
- ½ teaspn table-salt
- ¼ teaspn black pepper
- ½ cupsful vegetable oil

Cooking Instructions:

- In a large container, mix the sliced green and red cabbage with grated carrots.
- In another container, whisk apple cider vinegar, sugar, table-salt, Dijon mustard, black pepper, and celery seed till well combined.
- Gradually add the vegetable oil and whisk till the dressing is smooth and emulsified.
- Pour the dressing over the cabbage and carrot mixture, and toss till everything is coated evenly.
- Cover the container with plastic wrap and refrigerate for a minimum of 1 hour, or up to 24 hrs to allow the flavors to blend.
- Prior serving, give the coleslaw a quick stir, and adjust the seasoning with more table-salt and black pepper as needed.
- Serve the coleslaw chilled.

Note: Add minced parsley or green onions for extra flavor and color.

Smoked Corn

Smoked corn is a classic Texan side dish that's easy to prepare and perfect for any barbecue or summer cookout. The sweet and smoky flavor of the corn pairs perfectly with the tangy and spicy seasoning, making it a crowd-pleaser.

Prep Time: 15 mins

Cooking Duration: 2 hrs

Equipment:

- Smoker
- Wood chips (hickory or mesquite)
- Aluminum foil
- Tongs

Ingredients:

- 6 ears of fresh corn with the husks
- ¼ cupsful of butter, melted
- 2 tabspns brown sugar
- 1 tabspn chili grounded
- 1 teaspn garlic grounded
- 1 teaspn smoked paprika
- Black pepper and table-salt

Cooking Instructions:

- Prepare your smoker by foreheating it to 225° F. While waiting, soak your wood chips in water for at least 30 mins.
- In a small container, mix the melted butter, brown sugar, chili grounded, garlic, smoked paprika, and black pepper.
- Brush the butter mixture generously over each ear of corn, making sure to cover all sides.
- Wrap each ear of corn in aluminum foil, twisting the ends to seal them.
- When your smoker has reached the wanted temperature, add your wood chips to the coals.
- Position the wrapped corn on the grill grates using tongs to position them.
- Cover the smoker and smoke the corn around 2 hrs or till the kernels are fully cooked and tender.
- Once done, carefully withdraw the corn from the grill and unwrap them.
- Serve hot, and enjoy your delicious smoked corn as a side dish with your favorite barbecue meats.

Creamed corn

Creamed corn is a staple in Texas, and this recipe is a perfect example of how this classic side dish can be taken to the next level.

Preparatory Time: 15 mins

Duration: 20-25 mins

Equipment:

- Large frying pan
- Cutting board
- Sharp knife
- Mixing spoon
- Measuring cupsfuls and spoons

Ingredients:

- 4 cupsfuls fresh corn (between 4-5 ears.)
- 4 oz. softened cream cheese
- ¼ cupsful of heavy cream
- 2 seeded and finely minced jalapeño peppers
- 4 slices cooked, crumbled bacon
- 2 tabspns butter
- 1 tabspnsugar
- 1 teaspn garlic grounded
- Pepper and table-salt

Cooking Instructions:

- Start by cutting the kernels off the cobs of corn and setting them aside.
- Place your pan over medium heat, and melt butter. Add diced jalapeños and cook for 2-3 mins till they are soft.
- Next, add the corn to the pan and stir well. Cook for 5-7 mins, stirring occasionally till the corn is tender and lightly browned.
- Add cream cheese, heavy cream, sugar, garlic grounded, table-salt, and pepper and stir till combined.
- Lower the heat and let the mixture parboil for 8-10 mins, stirring occasionally till the creamed corn thickens.
- Bring down the pan and stir in crumbled bacon.
- Taste for seasoning and add as needed. Serve the creamed corn hot.

Texas-Style BBQ Sauce

Texas-style BBQ sauce is a tangy and spicy sauce perfect for smoky, slow-cooked meats like brisket, ribs, and chicken. The sauce is thick, rich, and slightly sweet, with a bold flavor that comes from a blend of chili grounded, tomato sauce, brown sugar, and vinegar. This sauce is a must-have at any backyard BBQ or cookout.

Prep Time: 10 mins

Cooking Duration: 45 mins

Equipment:

- Saucepan
- Whisk
- Measuring cupsfuls and spoons
- Wooden spoon

Ingredients:

- 1 cupsful ketchup
- ¼ cupsful brown sugar
- ¼ cupsful of apple cider vinegar
- ¼ cupsful of Worcestershire sauce
- 2 tabspns chili grounded
- 2 teaspns garlic grounded
- 1 teaspn onion grounded
- ½ teaspn black pepper
- ½ teaspn table-salt
- ¼ teaspn cayenne pepper
- ¼ cupsful water

Cooking Instructions:

- In a medium saucepan, mix ketchup, brown sugar, cider vinegar, Worcester sauce, grounded chili, garlic and onion grounded, black pepper, table-salt, and cayenne pepper till well combined.
- Using low heat, position the saucepan and stir in water to thin the sauce. Allow the mixture to a parboil, while you stir on occasions.
- Decrease the heat to low and let the sauce parboil for 45 mins, occasionally stirring till it thickens to the wanted consistency.
- Once the sauce has thickened, Withdraw the saucepan from the heat and let it cool for a few mins.
- Transfer the BBQ sauce to a jar and store it in an ice-box till ready to use.
- Serve the BBQ sauce with your favorite meats.

Note: If you prefer a spicier sauce, increase the amount of cayenne pepper or add a few drops of hot sauce. For a milder sauce, reduce the amount of chili grounded and cayenne pepper..

Texas-Style Green Beans

Texas-style green beans are a classic Southern side dish that pairs perfectly with any barbecue or Tex-Mex meal. The dish is prepared with bacon, onion, garlic, and canned green beans, which are slow-cooked to infuse the flavors.

Prep Time: 10 mins

Cooking Duration: 30 mins

Equipment:

- Large frying pan
- Wooden spoon or spatula
- Measuring cupsfuls and spoons
- Chopping board
- Cook's knife

Ingredients:

- 4 slices of diced bacon
- ½ onion, diced
- 2 cloves minced garlic
- 2 (14.5 oz) cans of drained green beans
- ½ cupsful of chicken broth
- ½ teaspn table-salt
- ¼ teaspn black chili

Cooking Instructions:

- On medium heat, position a wide fry-pan and add chopped bacon and cook till it's brittle around 5-7 mins.
- Using a spoon, withdraw the cooked bacon from the pan and Position it on a plate lined with paper towels to absorb excess fat.
- In the same fry-pan with the bacon fat, add diced onion and sauté till softened around 3-5 mins.
- Add minced garlic and cook for an extra 1-2 mins till fragrant.
- Add the drained green beans to the pan and stir to combine with the onion and garlic.
- Pour in chicken broth, black pepper, and table-salt, and stir well.
- Parboil mixture and cook for 15-20 mins. Stir it on occasions until the green beans are tender and the liquid has reduced.
- Pour back in the cooked bacon back to the fry-pan and stir.
- Serve the green beans hot.

Pinto Beans

Pinto beans are a staple of Texan cuisine and can be prepared in many ways

Prep Time: 10 mins

Cooking Duration: 2-3 hrs

Equipment:

- Use either a Braadpan or large pan that has a lid
- Chopping board
- Sharp knife
- Wooden spoon

Ingredients:

- 1 pound dry pinto beans
- 6 cupsfuls water
- 4 slices bacon, diced
- 1 semi-diced onion
- 2 cloves of minced garlic
- 2 teaspns chili grounded
- 1 teaspn cumin
- ½ teaspn smoked paprika
- ½ teaspn table-salt
- ¼ teaspn black pepper

Cooking Instructions:

- After rinsing the pinto beans in a colander, Withdraw any debris or stones.
- Using medium heat, add and cook diced bacon till its crispy. Using a slotted spoon, remove the bacon and set it aside, leaving the grease within the pan.
- Sauté diced onions in the pan till they become translucent and fragrant, about 5-7 mins. Then, cook minced garlic for 1-2 mins till fragrant.
- Add the rinsed pinto beans and combine with the onion and garlic.
- Stir in chili grounded, cumin, smoked paprika, and black pepper, and blend.
- Pour 6 cupsfuls of water and stir.
- Reduce the heat and allow the mixture to boil. Place a lid over the pan. Allow the beans to parboil for 2-3 hrs till they become very soft and the water has thickened.
- Add more water to cover the beans and continue to stir.
- Once the beans is soft to touch and the liquid has thickened, mix with the cooked bacon and serve hot.

Mac 'n Cheese

Mac' n Cheese is made with a combination of spicy jalapeños, smoky bacon, and a rich and creamy cheese sauce. This recipe is ideal for a cozy night or serving up at your next BBQ or panluck.

Prep Time: 20 mins

Cooking Duration: 30 mins

Equipment:

- Large pan
- Strainer
- Frying pan
- Oven-safe casserole dish
- Whisk

Ingredients:

- 1-pound elbow-macaroni
- 4 tabspns untable-salted butter
- 4 tabspns all-purpose flour
- 3 cupsfuls of whole milk
- 2 cupsfuls cheddar cheese shreds
- 1 cupsful of pepper jack cheese shreds
- ½ cupsful jalapeños (fresh or pickled), minced
- 6 slices of cooked and crumbled bacon
- ½ cupsful of panko breadcrumbs
- Pepper and table-salt

Cooking Instructions:

- Heat up your oven to 375° F.
- Boil the elbow macaroni in a large pan of generously table-salted water till it's firm. Drain the pasta in a strainer and set it aside.
- While the pasta is cooking, melt 4 tabspns of butter in a pan over medium heat. After the butter has melted, whisk in 4 tabspns of all-purpose flour to create a roux. Cook the roux, whisking constantly, for 1-2 mins till it begins to turn a golden brown hue.
- Gradually pour in 3 cupsfuls of whole milk, whisking constantly to avoid lumps from forming. Cook the milk blend for 5-7 mins, stirring regularly, till it thickens and coats the back of a spoon.
- Combine 2 cupsfuls of cheddar cheese shreds and 1 cupsful of pepper jack cheese shreds with the milk blend and stir till the cheese is fully melted and the sauce becomes smooth.
- Stir in ½ cupsful of diced jalapeños and 4 slices of crumbled bacon.
- Add in the cooked macaroni to the cheese sauce and stir till thoroughly combined. Then, flavor the dish with table-salt and pepper to taste.
- Transfer the mac 'n cheese to an oven-safe casserole dish.
- Sprinkle 2 slices of crumbled bacon and ½ cupsful of panko breadcrumbs over the top of the mac 'n cheese.
- Bake the mac 'n cheese in the foreheated oven for around 20-25 mins, or till the top becomes a golden brown color and the cheese begins to bubble.
- Give the mac 'n cheese a few mins to cool down prior serving. For an added touch, garnish with extra diced jalapeños and bacon..

Fried Okra

Fried okra is a popular Southern dish that has become a staple in Texan cuisine. This crispy and delicious side dish is perfect for any occasion, from barbecues to panlucks.

Prep Time: 15 mins

Cooking Duration: 20 mins

Equipment:

- Deep fry-pan or Braadpan
- Tongs
- Cutting board
- Knife
- Paper towels

Ingredients:

- 1 lb. fresh okra
- 1 cupsful of cornmeal
- 1 cupsful of all-purpose flour
- 1 tbsp. table-salt
- 1 teaspn black pepper
- 1 teaspn garlic grounded
- 1 teaspn onion grounded
- ½ teaspn cayenne pepper
- 2 large eggs
- ½ cupsful buttermilk
- Vegetable oil for frying

Cooking Instructions:

- Start by preparing the okra. Rinse it under cold water and pat it dry with paper towels. Cut off the ends and slice it into ½-inch pieces.
- In a large container, combine cornmeal, flour, table-salt, black pepper, garlic grounded, onion grounded, and cayenne pepper. Whisk everything together till well combined.
- Whisk together the eggs and buttermilk in a separate container.
- Dip each piece of okra into the egg mixture, shake off any excess liquid, and then coat it in the cornmeal mixture. Position the coated okra onto a plate or baking sheet.
- Heat about 1 inch of vegetable oil in a deep fry-pan or Braadpan over medium-high heat till it reaches 350°F.
- Using tongs, carefully add the coated okra to the hot oil. Fry the okra in batches, making sure not to overcrowd the pan. Fry for 2-3 mins or till the okra turns golden brown and crispy.
- Once the okra is fried, withdraw it from the oil and transfer it onto a plate to drain off any excess oil.
- Serve the fried okra hot, with your favorite dipping sauce on the side.

Collard Greens

Collard greens pair well with barbeque or any Texas-inspired meal. In this recipe, we'll use bacon, onion, and garlic to add depth and smokiness to the greens.

Prep Time: 15 mins

Cooking Duration: 1 hr 30 mins

Equipment:

- Large pan with a lid
- Large frying pan
- Cutting board
- Sharp knife
- Wooden spoon

Ingredients:

- 2 bunches of collard greens
- ½ pound diced bacon
- 1 medium diced onion
- 3 minced garlic cloves
- 3 cupsfuls vegetable or chicken broth
- ¼ cupsful of apple cider vinegar
- 2 tabspns brown sugar
- 1 tabspnsmoked paprika
- 1 teaspn cayenne pepper
- Pepper and table-salt

Cooking Instructions:

- Begin by preparing the collard greens. Rinse them thoroughly under running water and withdraw the tough stems from the center of the leaves. Roll the leaves up and then cut them into thin strips. Set aside.
- In a large frying pan, cook the diced bacon over medium heat till it becomes crispy. Once done, withdraw the bacon from the pan and set it aside. Add the diced onion and minced garlic to the same fry-pan and sauté till the onion becomes translucent and the garlic is fragrant.
- Add the collard greens to the onion and garlic and stir to combine.
- In a large pan, combine the chicken or vegetable broth, apple cider vinegar, brown sugar, smoked paprika, cayenne pepper, and a pinch of table-salt and pepper. Stir everything together.
- Add the collard green mixture to the pan with the cooked bacon and stir to combine.
- Bring the mixture to a boil over high heat, then reduce the heat to low, cover the pan with a lid, and parboil for 1 hour and 30 mins, stirring occasionally.
- After 1 hour and 30 mins, withdraw the lid and continue to parboil the collard greens for an extra 30 mins till the liquid reduces and thickens.
- Adjust the seasoning with table-salt and pepper according to your preference.
- Serve the collard greens hot as a side dish to accompany your favorite Texas meal.

Onion Rings

Onion rings are a classic snack that combines sweet onions and a crispy coating, making them an irresistible treat. They are a popular appetizer in Texas, often served alongside barbecue or fried foods.

Prep Time: 15 mins

Cooking Duration: 15-20 mins

Equipment:

- Deep fryer or heavy-bottomed pan
- Slotted spoon
- Containers
- Wire rack

Ingredients:

- 2 large sweet onions, sliced into Half-inch rounds
- 2 cupsfuls of all-purpose flour
- 1 tabspn garlic grounded
- 1 tabspn paprika
- 1 teaspn cayenne pepper
- 1 teaspn table-salt
- Half teaspn black pepper
- 2 cupsfuls buttermilk
- Vegetable oil

Cooking Instructions:

- Begin by foreheating your deep fryer or heavy-bottomed pan with 2-3 inches of vegetable oil to 375°F.
- In a large container, whisk together flour, garlic grounded, paprika, cayenne pepper, table-salt, and black pepper.
- In a separate container, pour in the buttermilk.
- Dip each onion slice into the flour mixture, then into the buttermilk, and then back into the flour mixture again. Make sure to press the flour mixture onto the onion to ensure it sticks.
- Once the oil is hot, carefully Position a few onion rings into the fryer using a slotted spoon. Fry for 2-3 mins or till golden brown.
- Use the slotted spoon to withdraw the onion rings from the oil and transfer them onto a wire rack to drain off any excess oil.
- Fry the remaining onion rings in batches to keep the oil temperature consistent.
- Serve the onion rings hot with your preferred dipping sauce.

Cheese Grits

Cheese grits are a classic and delicious Texas breakfast or brunch dish that is easy to make. This dish combines creamy grits with the sharpness of cheddar cheese and a touch of spice and creaminess.

Prep Time: 10 mins

Cooking Duration: 40 mins

Equipment:

- Medium-sized saucepan
- Whisk
- Wooden spoon
- Measuring cupsfuls and spoons
- Baking dish
- Oven

Ingredients:

- 1 cupsful stone-ground grits
- 4 cupsfuls of water
- 1 teaspn of table-salt
- Half teaspn of black pepper
- Qtr. teaspn of cayenne pepper
- 4 tabspns untable-salted butter
- Half cupsful of heavy cream
- 2 cupsfuls cheddar cheese shreds
- 2 large eggs, lightly beaten

Cooking Instructions:

- Foreheat your oven to 350°F (180°C).
- In a medium-sized saucepan, bring 4 cupsfuls of water to a boil. Add table-salt and grits while constantly whisking to prevent lumps from forming.
- Reduce the heat to low and allow the grits to parboil around 20-25 mins. Stir occasionally with a wooden spoon to ensure that they cook evenly and do not stick to the bottom of the pan. The grits should be soft and tender.
- Add the black pepper, cayenne pepper, butter, and heavy cream to the grits, stirring till everything is well combined.
- Withdraw the grits from heat and add shredded cheddar cheese, stirring vigorously till the cheese is melted and the mixture is smooth.
- Allow the mixture to cool slightly, and then add the lightly beaten eggs, stirring till well combined.
- Pour the grits mixture into a greased baking dish, and smooth the surface to create an even layer.
- Foreheat your oven and bake the grits around 15-20 mins, or till the top is golden brown and the mixture is set.
- Withdraw the baking dish from the oven and let it cool for a few mins prior serving.

Note: Add cooked bacon, sausage, or ham to the grits mixture prior baking for extra flavor and protein.

Stewed Cabbage

Stewed cabbage combines the sweetness of the cabbage with the smokiness of the bacon and the tanginess of vinegar.

Prep Time: 15 mins

Cooking Duration: 45 mins

Equipment:

- Large pan
- Knife
- Cutting board
- Spoon
- Tongs

Ingredients:

- 1 head cored and shredded green cabbage
- 4 slices of bacon, minced
- 1 onion, diced
- 3 cloves minced garlic
- 1 tabspn paprika
- 1 tabspn dried thyme
- 1 teaspn table-salt
- Half teaspn black pepper
- Half cupsful chicken broth
- Qtr. cupsful apple cider vinegar
- 2 tabspns brown sugar
- 2 tabspns untable-salted butter

Cooking Instructions:

- Begin by heating a large pan over medium heat. Add minced bacon and cook for 8-10 mins or till it becomes crispy. Use tongs to withdraw the bacon from the pan and set it aside.
- In the same pan, add diced onion to the bacon grease and cook till it becomes translucent, which usually takes 2-3 mins. Add minced garlic, paprika, thyme, black pepper, and table-salt to the pan and cook for a minute till it becomes fragrant.
- Add shredded cabbage to the onion and spice mixture and stir till combined. Cook the cabbage for 5-7 mins till it starts to wilt.
- Pour chicken broth, apple cider vinegar, brown sugar, and butter into the pan. Stir the ingredients together and bring the mixture to a parboil.
- Cover the pan and let the cabbage parboil for 30-35 mins or till it becomes tender and fully cooked. Make sure to stir the mixture occasionally.
- After the cabbage is fully cooked, taste it and adjust the seasoning if necessary. To serve, top the stewed cabbage with the crispy bacon crumbles and serve hot.

Baked Panato

Looking for a new twist on the classic panato salad recipe? Try making a baked panato salad!.This recipe includes baked panatoes instead of boiled, giving it a unique texture and flavor.

Prep Time: 20 mins

Cooking Duration: 1 hour 30 mins

Equipment:

- Oven
- Large container
- Small container
- Whisk
- Cutting board
- Knife
- Measuring cupsfuls and spoons
- Baking sheet

Ingredients:

- 6 large baking panatoes
- Half cupsful of mayonnaise
- Half cupsful of sour cream
- 1 tabspn yellow mustard
- Half teaspn garlic grounded
- Half teaspn onion grounded
- Half teaspn table-salt
- Qtr. teaspn black pepper
- 6 slices of cooked, crumbled bacon
- 1 cupsful cheddar cheese shreds
- 2 green thinly sliced onions

Cooking Instructions:

- Foreheat your oven to 400°F.
- Wash and scrub the panatoes. Take your panatoes and pierce them all over with a fork prior placing them on a baking sheet.
- Put the baking sheet with the panatoes in the oven and let them bake for 1 hour and 15 mins.
- While the panatoes are baking, take a small container and whisk together mayonnaise, sour cream, yellow mustard, garlic grounded, onion grounded, and black pepper. Set the container aside.
- Once the panatoes are done baking, let them cool down prior cutting them into bite-sized pieces and putting them in a large container.
- Add the bacon, shredded cheddar cheese, and green onions to the panatoes.
- Pour the mayonnaise mixture over the panato mixture and toss everything together till it's well combined.
- Refrigerate the panato salad for no less than 1 hour prior serving.

Pea Salad

Pea salad is a delicious and refreshing side dish perfect for any barbecue, picnic, or panluck gathering. It's made with sweet peas, bacon, cheddar cheese, and a tangy dressing, which gives it a creamy texture and a unique flavor.

Prep Time: 15 mins

Cooking Duration: 10 mins

Equipment:

- Large container
- Cutting board
- Chef's knife
- Frying pan
- Wooden spoon
- Measuring cupsfuls and spoons

Ingredients:

- 16 ounces frozen peas, thawed
- 6 slices of cooked and crumbled bacon
- Half cupsful diced cheddar cheese
- Qtr. cupsful diced red onion
- Qtr. cupsful diced celery
- Half cupsful mayonnaise
- Qtr. cupsful sour cream
- 1 tabspn p apple cider vinegar
- 1 tabspn Dijon mustard
- Qtr. teaspn garlic grounded
- Pepper and table-salt

Cooking Instructions:

- In a large container, combine the thawed peas, crumbled bacon, diced cheddar cheese, red onion, and celery. Toss everything together to combine.
- In a small pan, cook the bacon till it becomes crispy over medium heat. Once cooked, put the bacon on a plate lined with paper towel to drain.
- In a small container, whisk together the mayonnaise, apple cider vinegar, sour cream, garlic grounded, pepper, Dijon mustard and table-salt till everything is well combined.
- Pour the dressing over the pea mixture and stir everything together till it's evenly coated.
- To allow the flavors to meld, cover the container with plastic wrap and refrigerate for at least 1 hour.
- Give the salad a quick stir and garnish with extra bacon crumbles if wanted prior serving. Serve chilled or at room temperature.

Chapter 3: Loving Tacos & Tex-Mex

Chimichangas

Chimichangas is the Texan version of the Mexican quesadilla. These delicious handheld treats are a deep-fried crispy flour tortilla filled with a series of ingredients.

Prep Time: 20 mins

Cooking Duration: 15 mins

Equipment:

- Large frying pan
- Container
- Spoon
- Deep fryer or large frying pan
- Tongs
- Paper towels
- Baking sheet

Ingredients:

- 2 cupsfuls of cooked chicken shreds
- ½ cupsful of diced onion
- ½ cupsful of diced green bell pepper
- ½ cupsful of diced red bell pepper
- 1 teaspn ground cumin
- 1 teaspn chili grounded
- Pepper and table-salt
- 1 cupsful cheddar cheese shredded
- 8 large flour tortillas
- Vegetable oil for frying

Cooking Instructions:

- In a large pan, sauté the minced onion, green and red bell pepper till they become tender.
- Add the cooked and shredded chicken to the fry-pan and season it with cumin, chili grounded, table-salt, and pepper. Mix everything together evenly and cook for an extra 5 mins till the chicken is heated through.
- Withdraw the fry-pan from the heat and let the chicken mixture cool down slightly.
- Foreheat the deep fryer or a large pan filled with vegetable oil to 350°F (180°C).
- Assemble the chimichangas by placing a spoonful of the chicken mixture and shredded cheddar cheese onto a flour tortilla.
- Fold the tortilla sides in the center and then roll it up tightly.
- Use tongs to carefully Position the chimichangas into the hot oil and fry both sides for 2-3 mins or till they become golden brown and crispy.
- Use tongs to withdraw the chimichangas from the oil and then Position them on a baking sheet lined with paper towel to drain off any excess oil.
- Serve the chimichangas hot alongside your preferred toppings, such as guacamole, salsa, and sour cream.

Puffy Tacos

Puffy tacos are a unique Tex-Mex specialty that involves frying tortillas till they puff up and become crispy. These tacos are typically filled with a variety of savory ingredients, such as beef, chicken, or beans, and then topped with fresh vegetables and salsa.

Prep Time: 20 mins

Cooking Duration: 30 mins

Equipment:

- Large frying pan
- Tongs
- Medium saucepan
- Deep-fry thermostat
- Slotted spoon
- Paper towels

Ingredients:

- 1 pound ground beef
- 1 teaspn chili grounded
- 1 teaspn cumin
- 1 teaspn paprika
- ½ teaspn garlic grounded
- ½ teaspn onion grounded
- ½ teaspn table-salt
- ¼ teaspn black pepper
- ¼ teaspn cayenne pepper
- ½ cupsful beef broth
- 12 corn tortillas
- Vegetable oil, for frying
- Shredded lettuce
- Diced tomatoes
- Shredded cheese

Cooking Instructions:

- In a large frying pan, heat the ground beef over medium-high heat till it is fully cooked and no longer pink.
- Add the chili grounded, cumin, paprika, garlic and onion grounded, black pepper, and then cayenne pepper to the frying pan, after draining its excess fat. Stir to combine.
- Combine the beef broth with the beef mixture and let it parboil for 10-15 mins.
- While the beef mixture is parboiling, pour about 1 inch of vegetable oil into a medium-sized saucepan and Position it over medium-high heat. Use a deep-fry thermostat to monitor the oil temperature, and heat it to 375°F.
- Gently Position a corn tortilla into the hot oil using tongs. Press down on the tortilla with the tongs till it becomes puffy and crispy, which should take roughly 30 seconds.
- Flip the tortilla over using the tongs and fry the other side till it is crispy as well, which should take another 30 seconds.

- Withdraw the fried tortilla from the oil using a slotted spoon and transfer it to a plate lined with paper towels to Withdraw excess oil. Repeat the process with the remaining tortillas.
- Spoon some of the beef mixture into each fried tortilla shell to assemble the tacos. Top with diced tomatoes, shredded lettuce, and cheese shreds.

Fajitas

Fajitas are a delicious Tex-Mex dish that can be enjoyed any day of the week. They are typically prepared with grilled strips of meat, onions, and peppers, all wrapped in a warm flour tortilla.

Prep Time: 20 mins

Cooking Duration: 15-20 mins

Equipment:

- Large fry-pan or grill pan
- Tongs
- Cutting board
- Chef's knife

Ingredients:

- 1 lb. of beef or chicken (thinly sliced into strips)
- 1 onion (thinly sliced into strips)
- 2 bell peppers (thinly sliced into strips)
- 2 cloves of minced garlic
- 2 tabspns vegetable oil
- 1 teaspn chili grounded
- 1 teaspn cumin
- Pepper and table-salt
- Flour tortillas
- Toppings of your choice (sour cream, guacamole, or salsa)

Cooking Instructions:

- Heat a large frying or grill pan over medium-high heat.
- Thinly slice the meat, onion, and peppers.
- In a small container, mix the chili grounded, cumin, table-salt, and pepper.
- Once the pan is hot, add vegetable oil followed by the sliced meat and garlic. Cook for 3-4 mins till the meat is browned.
- Next, add the sliced onion and peppers to the pan and cook for an extra 5-7 mins, stirring occasionally till the vegetables are tender and the meat is fully cooked.
- Sprinkle the spice mixture onto the meat and vegetables and stir to combine.
- Warm up the flour tortillas according to the package Cooking Instructions.
- Serve the fajita mixture on the warm tortillas, and top with your favorite sauce, such as sour cream, guacamole, and salsa.

Salsa Verde Beef Tacos

Salsa verde beef tacos are a delicious and easy-to-make Mexican-inspired dish that is perfect for any weeknight dinner or weekend fiesta.

Prep Time: 15 mins

Cooking Duration: 30 mins

Equipment:

- Oven
- Big frying pan
- Tongs
- Cutting board
- Chef's knife
- Blender or food processor
- Container

Ingredients:

- 1 lb. beef (flank steak or skirt steak)
- 8-10 small corn tortillas
- ¼ cupsful olive oil
- ¼ cupsful fresh cilantro, minced
- ¼ cupsful fresh lime juice
- 1 seeded and minced jalapeno pepper
- 2 minced cloves of garlic
- ½ teaspn cumin
- ½ teaspn table-salt
- ¼ teaspn black pepper

Cooking Instructions:

- Set the oven to medium-high heat and foreheat a large frying pan.
- In a container, combine 2 tabspns of olive oil, table-salt, and black pepper. Rub the mixture all over the beef.
- Foreheat a fry-pan over medium-high heat. Once hot, Position the beef in the pan and cook for 3-4 mins per side till browned and cooked to your wanted level of doneness.
- Withdraw the beef from the pan and cool for 5 mins. Once cooled, use a sharp knife to slice it thinly across the grain.
- While the beef is cooling, prepare the salsa verde. In a blender or food processor, combine 2 tabspns of olive oil, cilantro, lime juice, jalapeno pepper, garlic, cumin, table-salt, and black pepper. Blend till smooth.
- In a container, toss the sliced beef with the salsa verde till fully coated.
- Warm up the tortillas in the microwave or in a separate frying pan.
- Assemble the tacos by placing a few slices of beef in the center of each tortilla. Top with extra salsa verde, if wanted, and serve immediately.

Cilantro Lime Chicken Tacos

Cilantro lime chicken tacos consist of juicy chicken breasts marinated in a zesty and citrusy cilantro lime marinade, then grilled to perfection and served in warm tortillas with your favorite toppings.

Prep Time: 15 mins

Cooking Duration: 15 mins

Equipment:

- Grill or grill pan
- Container
- Ziplock bag
- Tongs
- Cutting board
- Knife

Ingredients:

- 4 skinless, boneless chicken breasts
- 2 limes, juiced (about ¼ cupsful)
- ¼ cupsful minced fresh cilantro
- 2 minced cloves of garlic
- 2 tabspns olive oil
- 1 teaspn ground cumin
- ½ teaspn chili grounded
- Pepper and table-salt
- Tortillas
- Toppings: diced avocado, diced tomatoes, sliced jalapeños, shredded cheese, sour cream, etc.

Cooking Instructions:

- In a container, whisk together lime juice, cilantro, garlic, olive oil, cumin, chili grounded, table-salt, and pepper.
- Position chicken breasts in a large ziplock bag, pour the marinade over the chicken, and seal the bag. Refrigerate for at least 30 mins, or up to 2 hrs.
- Foreheat a grill or grill pan over medium-high heat.
- Withdraw the chicken from the marinade, and discard the remaining marinade.
- Grill the chicken for 5-6 mins per side, or till cooked through and no longer pink in the center. Flip the chicken using tongs.
- Withdraw the chicken from the grill and cool for 5 mins prior slicing.
- Warm tortillas in the microwave or on a hot pan.
- Slice the chicken into thin strips or bite-sized pieces.
- Assemble the tacos by placing the chicken on the tortillas and adding your wanted toppings.
- Serve and enjoy!

Grilled Chicken Taco with Feta Cream

The combination of grilled chicken, fresh vegetables, and feta cream creates a mouth-watering taco that will satisfy your hunger and taste buds.

Prep Time: 15 mins

Cooking Duration: 20 mins

Equipment:

- Grill or grill pan
- Container
- Cutting board
- Knife
- Measuring cupsfuls and spoons
- Tongs

Ingredients:

- 1 pound chicken breasts
- 1 tabspn taco seasoning
- 1 tabspn olive oil
- Pepper and table-salt
- 6-8 taco shells
- ½ cupsful feta cheese crumbles
- ½ cupsful sour cream
- 1 tabspn lime juice
- ¼ cupsful fresh minced cilantro
- ½ cupsful diced tomatoes
- ½ cupsful diced red onion
- ½ cupsful lettuce shreds

Cooking Instructions:

- Over medium-high heat, foreheat the grill or grill pan.
- Start by mixing together taco seasoning, olive oil, table-salt, and pepper in a container.
- Coat chicken breasts evenly with the seasoning mixture and Position them on the grill.
- Grill the chicken on both sides for 10-12 mins or till the core temperature reaches 165°F.
- Withdraw chicken from the grill and cool for a few mins, then slice it into small pieces.
- In a separate container, mix together feta cheese, sour cream, lime juice, and cilantro to create a creamy topping. Set it aside.
- According to package Cooking Instructions, warm the taco shells in the oven or microwave.
- Fill each taco shell with the sliced chicken, diced tomatoes, diced red onion, shredded lettuce, and a dollop of feta cream.

Carnitas

Carnitas is a flavorful and juicy Tex-Mex pork dish that is slow-cooked till it is tender and falls apart easily.

Prep Time: 15 mins

Cooking Duration: 4-6 hrs

Equipment:

- Slow cooker or Braadpan
- Cutting board
- Sharp knife
- Measuring spoons and cupsfuls
- Tongs
- Big container

Ingredients:

- 3-4 lbs trimmed pork shoulder cut into large chunks
- 2 tabspns vegetable oil
- 1 teaspn table-salt
- 1 teaspn chili grounded
- 1 teaspn cumin
- 1 teaspn garlic grounded
- 1 teaspn oregano
- ½ teaspn paprika
- ½ teaspn black pepper
- 1 orange juice
- 1 lime juice
- 1 onion, minced
- 4 minced garlic cloves
- 1 jalapeño pepper, seeded and minced
- ½ cupsful chicken broth

Cooking Instructions:

- Combine table-salt, chili grounded, cumin, garlic grounded, oregano, paprika, and black pepper in a large container.
- Add pork shoulder chunks and toss till evenly coated with the spice mixture.
- Heat vegetable oil in a pan over medium-high heat. Add pork chunks in batches and cook for 3-4 mins per side till browned on all sides.
- Transfer the browned pork chunks to a slow cooker or Braadpan.
- In the same frying pan, cook jalapeño pepper, minced onion, and minced garlic till softened and lightly browned.
- Pour orange and lime juice over the pork, then add the cooked onion mixture on top.
- Pour chicken broth over the pork and vegetables.
- Cook on low heat for 6-8 hrs or high for 4-6 hrs till the meat is tender and falls apart easily. If using a Braadpan, cook covered in a foreheated 325°F oven for 3-4 hrs or till the meat is tender.
- Withdraw pork chunks from the slow cooker or Braadpan and Position them on a cutting board.
- Shred the pork using two forks and hand it back it to the cooking liquid.

- Serve the Tex-Mex Carnitas in tacos, burritos, or on top of nachos. Garnish with fresh cilantro, minced onion, and lime wedges.

Beef Picadillo

Beef Picadillo is a delicious and flavorful dish that combines ground beef with a blend of spices and vegetables. The dish is simple to prepare and can be served with rice, tortillas, or as a filling for tacos.

Prep Time: 15 mins

Cooking Duration: 30 mins

Equipment:

- Large frying pan
- Knife
- Cutting board
- Wooden spoon

Ingredients:

- 1 lb. ground beef
- 1 onion, diced
- 2 cloves garlic, minced
- 1 green bell pepper, diced
- 1 red bell pepper, diced
- 1 seeded and diced jalapeno pepper
- 1 can diced tomatoes (14.5 oz)
- 1 can tomato sauce (8 oz)
- 1 tabspn chili grounded
- 1 teaspn ground cumin
- 1 teaspn dried oregano
- Pepper and table-salt
- ¼ cupsful minced fresh cilantro

Cooking Instructions:

- Position a large pan over medium-high heat. Cook the ground beef in the pan, breaking it into small pieces as it browns, till fully cooked.
- Add in the green bell pepper, red bell pepper, jalapeno pepper, onion, and garlic to the pan with the beef. Cook and stir for 5-7 mins till the vegetables have softened.
- Mix together the chili grounded, cumin, oregano, table-salt, pepper, diced tomatoes, and tomato sauce. Stir to combine.
- Reduce the heat to low and let the mixture parboil for 20-25 mins, or till the sauce thickens and the flavors have blended together.
- Prior serving, add the minced cilantro and stir well.
- Serve the beef picadillo hot, either as a main dish or with rice, tortillas, or as a filling for tacos.

Fish Tacos

Fish tacos are a popular dish in Tex-Mex cuisine. These tacos are made with crispy fried fish, fresh vegetables, and a flavorful sauce.

Prep Time: 20 mins

Cooking Duration: 15 mins

Equipment:

- Large frying pan
- Container
- Tongs
- Cutting board
- Knife

Ingredients:

For the Fish:

- 1-pound cod fillets
- ½ cupful of all-purpose flour
- ½ teaspn cumin
- ½ teaspn chili grounded
- ½ teaspn garlic grounded
- ½ teaspn table-salt
- ¼ teaspn black pepper
- ½ cupful of beer
- ½ cupful vegetable oil

For the Tacos:

- 8 corn tortillas
- 1 cupful shredded cabbage
- ¼ cupful minced cilantro
- ¼ cupful diced red onion
- ½ cupful diced tomato
- 1 avocado, diced
- Lime wedges, for serving

For the Sauce:

- ½ cupful of sour cream
- ¼ cupful of mayonnaise
- 1 tabspn lime juice
- ½ teaspn cumin
- ½ teaspn chili grounded
- ¼ teaspn table-salt

Cooking Instructions:

- In a container, mix together the flour, cumin, chili grounded, garlic grounded, table-salt, and black pepper till well combined.

- Gradually add in the beer, stirring continuously, till a smooth batter forms.

- Cut the cod fillets into bite-sized pieces.

- In a large frying pan, heat vegetable oil over medium-high heat.

- Dip each fish piece into the batter, ensuring that they are evenly coated.

- Gently Position the battered fish in the hot oil using tongs.

- Fry for roughly 2-3 mins on each side or till the fish turns golden brown and crispy.

- Transfer the cooked fish to a paper towel-lined plate to drain excess oil.

- In a small container, whisk together sour cream, mayonnaise, lime juice, cumin, and chili grounded to make the sauce. Set aside.

- Warm the corn tortillas in a dry fry-pan over medium heat for 1-2 mins on each side.

- Assemble the tacos by placing a few pieces of the crispy fish on each tortilla. Top with shredded cabbage, cilantro, red onion, diced tomato, and avocado.

- Drizzle the sauce over the top of each taco and add lime wedges on the side when serving.

Barbacoa Taco

Barbacoa is a Tex-Mex dish consisting of beef or lamb slow-cooked in a pit or in a covered pan with spices and seasonings. The meat is tender and flavorful, and it's perfect for tacos, burritos, or served on its own.

Prep Time: 15 mins

Cooking Duration: 6-8 hrs

Equipment:

- Slow cooker
- Container
- Chef's knife
- Cutting board
- Tongs
- Measuring cupsfuls and spoons

Ingredients:

For the beef:

- 3 pounds beef chuck roast
- ¼ cupsful apple cider vinegar
- 3 tabspns tomato paste
- 3 tabspns chili grounded
- 1 tabspn ground cumin
- 1 tabspn dried oregano
- 1 teaspn smoked paprika
- 1 teaspn table-salt
- ½ teaspn black pepper
- 4 cloves garlic, minced
- ½ onion, minced
- ¼ cupsful beef broth

For the tacos:

- 12-16 small tortillas
- ½ onion, diced
- Fresh cilantro, minced
- Lime wedges
- Salsa or hot sauce for serving

Cooking Instructions:

- Mix together the apple cider vinegar, tomato paste, chili grounded, ground cumin, dried oregano, smoked paprika, table-salt, black pepper, garlic, and onion in a container, and stir till a paste forms.
- Cut the beef chuck roast into large chunks, about 2-3 inches in size. On the slow cooker, add the beef chunks.
- Pour the spice paste over the beef, making sure all the pieces are coated evenly.
- Pour the beef broth into the slow cooker and gently mix it in with the meat and spice mixture.

- Cover the slow cooker and cook on low heat for 6-8 hrs, or till the beef is tender and easily shredded.

- Using tongs, withdraw the beef from the slow cooker and shred it with a fork.

- Warm the tortillas in a pan or in the oven to assemble the tacos.

- Fill each tortilla with shredded beef, diced onion, and minced cilantro.

- Top with a squeezed wedge of lime and serve with salsa or hot sauce on the side.

Chili Con Carne

Chili con carne is a real classic Tex-Mex dish that's perfect for any occasion. It's a stew made with cubed beef, chili peppers, onions, and spices, giving it a bold and spicy flavor. This dish is traditionally served with rice, cornbread, or tortilla chips.

Prep Time: 20 mins

Cooking Duration: 1 hr 30 mins

Equipment:

- Large pan or Braadpan
- Cutting board
- Knife
- Wooden spoon or spatula

Ingredients:

- 2 lbs cubed beef (chuck or round)
- 2 tabspn vegetable oil
- 1 large diced onion
- 4 garlic minced cloves
- 2 tabspn chili grounded
- 1 tabspn ground cumin
- 1 teaspn of smoked paprika
- ½ teaspn of cayenne pepper
- ½ teaspn of black pepper
- ½ teaspn of table-salt
- 2 cupsfuls beef broth
- ½ cupsful water
- 2 tabspn cornmeal

Cooking Instructions:

- Using a Braadpan, heat the vegetable oil over medium-high heat.
- Add cubed beef and brown on all sides, then Withdraw and set aside.
- Next, cook minced garlic and diced onion in the same pan for 2-3 mins till onion is soft, stirring occasionally.
- Stir in ground cumin, chili grounded, smoked paprika, cayenne pepper, black pepper, and table-salt till well combined with the onions and garlic.
- Pour in beef broth and water together, stirring to combine.
- Hand it back the browned beef to the pan, making sure it's coated with the spices and liquid.
- Parboil the mixture by decreasing heat to low, then cover the pan and cook for 1 hour, stirring occasionally to prevent sticking.
- After 1 hour, uncover the pan. To allow the liquid to thicken, continue cooking for an extra 30 mins
- Whisk together cornmeal and ¼ cupsful of water in a small container till smooth.
- Add cornmeal mixture to the pan and stir to combine, then cook till chili has thickened to your wanted consistency, usually an extra 10-15 mins.
- Withdraw from heat and let sit for 10-15 mins prior serving.

Hard Tacos

Hard Tacos are a classic Tex-Mex version of the Mexican soft tacos. The taco shells are fried till crispy and filled with seasoned ground beef, lettuce, cheese, tomatoes, and sour cream.

Prep Time: 10 mins

Cooking Duration: 20 mins

Equipment:

- Large frying pan
- Tongs
- Paper towels
- Baking sheet
- Oven

Ingredients:

- 12 corn tortillas
- Vegetable oil, for frying
- 1 pound ground beef
- 1 tabspn chili grounded
- 1 teaspn cumin
- ½ teaspn garlic grounded
- ½ teaspn onion grounded
- ½ teaspn kashering table-salt
- ¼ teaspn black pepper
- ½ cupsful water
- Shredded lettuce
- Cheddar cheese shreds
- Diced tomatoes
- Sour cream

Cooking Instructions:

- Foreheat your oven to 350° F.
- Heat 1 tabspn of vegetable oil in a pan over medium-high heat.
- Carefully Position one corn tortilla in the hot oil using tongs. Fry for around 30 seconds and then fold it in half to create a taco shape. Use the tongs to hold the tortilla in Position as you fry it for another 30 seconds. Flip the tortilla and fry for another 30 seconds on the other side till crispy and lightly browned.
- Withdraw the taco shell from the oil with tongs and drain excess oil on a paper towel-lined baking sheet. Repeat the process with the remaining tortillas.
- In another frying pan, cook the ground beef over medium-high heat till browned.
- Add chili grounded, cumin, garlic grounded, onion grounded, table-salt, black pepper, and water to the fry-pan with the ground beef. Stir to combine and let parboil for 5-10 mins.
- To assemble the tacos, spoon a generous portion of the ground beef into each taco shell.
- Top the beef with shredded lettuce, shredded cheddar cheese, diced tomatoes, and a dollop of sour cream.

- Position the filled taco shells back on the baking sheet and bake for 5-10 mins inside the oven till the cheese is melted and the taco shells are heated through.
- Serve and enjoy!

Guacamole

Guacamole is a classic Tex-Mex dip made with mashed ripe avocados, lime juice, table-salt, and other ingredients like onion, tomato, cilantro, and jalapeño peppers.

Prep Time: 10 mins

Cooking Duration: 10 mins

Equipment:

- Knife
- Cutting board
- Fork or panato masher
- Container

Ingredients:

- 3 ripe avocados
- 1 small finely minced onion
- 1 small minced tomato
- 1 seeded and finely minced jalapeño pepper
- ¼ cupsful minced fresh cilantro
- 2 tabspns fresh lime juice
- Ground black pepper and table-salt

Cooking Instructions:

- Start by cutting the avocados in half lengthwise and removing the pit. Scoop out the flesh and transfer it to a container.
- Using a fork, mash the avocado till it's mostly smooth with a few small chunks remaining.
- Add the minced onion, tomato, jalapeño pepper, and cilantro to the container with the mashed avocado.
- Drizzle lime juice over the mixture, then add table-salt and black pepper to taste.
- Mix all the ingredients together till well combined.
- Taste the guacamole and adjust the seasoning as needed.
- Refrigerate covered till ready to serve or serve immediately with tortilla chips.

Yellow Cheese Enchiladas

Tex-Mex enchiladas is made with ground beef, corn tortillas, enchilada sauce, and features the yellow cheese versus the Mexican white cheese.

Prep Time: 20 mins

Cooking Duration: 35 mins

Equipment:

- Large frying pan
- Baking dish
- Oven
- Container
- Aluminum foil

Ingredients:

- 1-pound cooked and ground beef
- 1 can of enchilada sauce
- 12 corn tortillas
- 2 cupsfuls yellow cheese shreds
- 1 diced onion
- 2 minced garlic cloves
- 1 tabspn of olive oil
- Pepper and table-salt
- Cilantro, minced (optional)

Cooking Instructions:

- Foreheat your oven to 350°F.
- In a large fry-pan set over medium heat, warm up some olive oil. Add minced garlic and diced onions and sauté till the onions turn translucent.
- Add a pound of beef to the pan and season it with table-salt and pepper. Cook for 2-3 mins, stirring occasionally, till the meat is heated through.
- Pour enchilada sauce into the fry-pan and stir till the beef is coated in the sauce.
- Spread a thin layer of the beef and sauce mixture on the bottom of a baking dish.
- Scoop some of the beef mixture onto the center of a corn tortilla. Roll the tortilla up and Position it seam-side down into the baking dish. Repeat with the remaining beef mixture and tortillas.
- Pour the remaining sauce over the rolled tortillas in the baking dish.
- Sprinkle shredded yellow cheese over the top of the sauce.
- Cover the baking dish with aluminum foil and bake around 25 mins.
- Withdraw the foil and bake for an extra 5-10 mins, or till the cheese is melted and bubbly.
- Withdraw the dish from the oven and let it cool for a few mins prior serving.
- Garnish with minced cilantro (optional) and serve hot.

Burritos

Tex-Mex Burritos are a delicious and filling meal made with a large tortilla filled with a variety of ingredients such as rice, beans, cheese, meat, and vegetables.

Prep Time: 30 mins

Cooking Duration: 30 mins

Equipment:

- Large frying pan
- Pan for cooking rice
- Cutting board
- Knife
- Container
- Tortilla warmer or foil

Ingredients:

- 1 pound ground beef
- 1 tabspn chili grounded
- 1 teaspn ground cumin
- ½ teaspn garlic grounded
- ¼ teaspn cayenne pepper
- ½ teaspn table-salt
- ¼ teaspn black pepper
- 1 teaspn olive oil
- ½ cupsful onion, minced
- ½ cupsful green pepper, minced
- 1 cupsful cooked rice
- 1 cupsful drained canned black beans
- 1 cupsful shredded cheddar cheese
- 6 large flour tortillas
- Salsa and sour cream for serving

Cooking Instructions:

- Heat a large fry-pan over medium-high heat and add the ground beef. Cook the beef till it is browned. Break it up into pieces as it cooks. Drain off any excess fat.
- Mix chili grounded, cayenne and black pepper, cumin, garlic grounded, and table-salt in a container. Add the spice mixture to the cooked ground beef in a fry-pan and stir to coat the meat.
- Add diced onion, green pepper, and olive oil to the fry-pan with the beef. Cook till the vegetables are softened.
- Stir in the cooked rice and black beans and cook for 2-3 mins, or till everything is heated through.
- Warm the tortillas in a tortilla warmer or wrapped in foil in the oven for a few mins.
- Position a tortilla on a plate and spoon some of the filling mixture down the center of the tortilla. Top with shredded cheese.
- Fold the sides of the tortilla over the filling and roll up tightly to create a burrito. Do same with the cool of the tortillas and filling.
- Serve the burritos with sour cream and salsa on the side.

Nachos

Nachos is an easy-to-make snack that can be customized with your favorite toppings. This recipe includes classic toppings like ground beef, cheese, beans, and fresh vegetables.

Prep Time: 10 mins

Cooking Duration: 20 mins

Equipment:

- Oven
- Baking sheet
- Frying pan
- Container
- Spatula

Ingredients:

- 1 bag of tortilla chips
- 1-pound ground beef
- 1 can of beans, refried
- 1 cupsful shredded cheddar cheese
- ½ cupsful diced tomatoes
- ½ cupsful diced onions
- ½ cupsful sliced black olives
- 1 jalapeno pepper, sliced (optional)
- 1 tabspn chili grounded
- 1 teaspn garlic grounded
- 1 teaspn cumin
- Pepper and table-salt

Cooking Instructions:

- Prewarm your oven to 375°F (190°C).
- Heat a fry-pan over medium heat and add the ground beef. Cook till it is browned and no longer pink. Drain excess fat.
- Add chili grounded, garlic grounded, cumin, table-salt, and pepper to the cooked ground beef. Stir to incorporate.
- In a container, combine refried beans with Qtr. cupsful of water. Mix till smooth.
- In one layer on a baking sheet, arrange the tortilla chips.
- Spoon the refried beans over the tortilla chips, spreading them evenly.
- Sprinkle the ground beef on top of the beans.
- Top with shredded cheese, diced tomatoes, onions, black olives, and jalapeno pepper (if using).
- Bake in the oven till the moment the cheese is melted and bubbly, usually 10-15 mins.
- Allow the dish to cool for a few mins prior serving while still hot.

Queso Dip

Queso dip is a creamy and cheesy dip made with melted cheese, jalapenos and spicy diced tomatoes.

Prep Time: 10 mins

Cooking Duration: 10 mins

Equipment:

- Medium saucepan
- Wooden spoon
- Cutting board
- Knife

Ingredients:

- 2 tabspns untable-salted butter
- 2 tabspns all-purpose flour
- 1 cupsful milk
- 1 cupsful cheddar cheese shreds
- 1 cupsful Monterey Jack cheese shred
- 1 can diced, drained tomatoes with green chilies
- ¼ cupsful diced jalapenos
- Table-salt

Cooking Instructions:

- In a medium saucepan, melt the butter over medium heat.
- Add the flour and stir with a wooden spoon till well combined.
- Gradually whisk in the milk to the saucepan, whisking constantly to prevent lumps.
- Continue cooking and stirring till the mixture comes to a boil and thickens, about 5-7 mins.
- On low heat, add the shredded cheddar and Monterey Jack cheeses to the sauce and stir till melted and smooth.
- Stir in the drained diced tomatoes with green chilies and diced jalapenos till well combined.
- Taste the queso dip and add table-salt as needed.
- Keep the queso dip warm over low heat till ready to serve.
- Serve with tortilla chips or your favorite dipping food.

Tamales

Tamales are a traditional Tex-Mex filled with spicy meat and cheese and wrapped in a corn husk. They are steamed to perfection and served with salsa and guacamole on the side.

Prep Time: 2 hrs

Cooking Duration: 2 hrs

Equipment:

- Large pan
- Steamer basket
- Containers
- Electric mixer
- Large mixing spoon
- Measuring cupsfuls and spoons
- Sharp knife
- Cutting board

Ingredients:

For filling:

- 1 lb. ground beef
- 1 small finely minced onion
- 2 cloves minced garlic
- 2 tabspns chili grounded
- 1 teaspn ground cumin
- 1 teaspn paprika
- 1 teaspn table-salt
- ½ teaspn. black pepper
- ½ cupsful tomato sauce
- ½ cupsful chicken broth
- 1 cupsful shredded cheddar cheese

For the masa:

- 3 cupsfuls masa harina
- 1 ½ cupsfuls chicken broth
- 1 teaspn baking grounded
- 1 teaspn table-salt
- ½ cupsful lard or vegetable shortening
- 1 cupsful of water

For assembly:

- Position dried corn husks in a container and cover with warm water. Soak for at least 30 mins.
- Salsa and guacamole

Cooking Instructions:

- Foreheat a large pan over medium-high heat to cook the beef filling. Brown the ground beef, garlic, and onion till the beef is fully cooked and the onion is tender.

- Mix the chili grounded, black pepper, cumin, paprika, and table-salt in a container, then add it to the fry-pan and stir.

- Pour the tomato sauce and chicken broth into the fry-pan and stir till well combined. Parboil and cook for 5-10 mins, or till the sauce has slightly thickened.

- Withdraw the pan from heat and add the shredded cheddar cheese. Set aside.

- In a large container, combine the masa harina, baking grounded, and table-salt to make the masa.

- In a separate container, use an electric mixer to beat the lard or vegetable shortening till light and fluffy. Then, add it to the masa harina mixture and stir.

- Gradually pour the chicken broth and water into the mixture, stirring till it forms a smooth dough.

- Lay a soaked corn husk on a flat surface to assemble the tamales. Spoon a tabspn of the masa onto the husk and spread it out to form a rectangle.

- Position a tabspn of the beef filling in the center of the masa rectangle.

- Roll the tamale tightly, using the corn husk to wrap it up. Fold the bottom of the husk up and secure it with a piece of kitchen twine.

- Do same with the remaining corn husks, masa, and filling till all of the tamales are assembled.

- Steam the tamales in a steamer basket or till the masa is firm and the filling is hot, usually 1 ½ to 2 hrs.

- Serve the tamales hot with salsa and guacamole on the side.

Chiles Rellenos

Tex-Mex Chiles Rellenos is a classic dish that's popular for its spicy and savory flavor. It's made by stuffing roasted poblano peppers with a mixture of cheese, meat, or vegetables and then coated in an egg batter prior being fried to a golden crisp.

Prep Time: 30 mins

Cooking Duration: 30 mins

Equipment:

- Baking sheet
- Aluminum foil
- Cutting board
- Knife
- Container
- Hand mixer or whisk
- Large frying pan
- Tongs
- Paper towels

Ingredients:

- 6 large poblano peppers
- 1 cupsful Monterey Jack cheese shred
- ½ cupsful cooked and crumbled chorizo
- ½ cupsful of all-purpose flour
- 1 teaspn baking grounded
- ½ teaspn table-salt
- 3 eggs, separated
- ¼ cupsful milk
- Vegetable oil for frying

Cooking Instructions:

- Foreheat your oven to 400°F.
- Cover a baking sheet with aluminum foil.
- Roast the poblano peppers on the prepared baking sheet in the oven for 15-20 mins, turning occasionally, till charred and blistered.
- Transfer the roasted peppers to a container and cover with plastic wrap. Cool for 10 mins.
- Withdraw the stem, skin, and seeds from the peppers. Rinse any remaining seeds under cold water and pat dry with paper towels.
- Mix shredded cheese and crumbled chorizo in a container.
- Stuff each poblano pepper with the cheese and chorizo mixture, being careful not to overstuff them.
- Mix together flour, baking grounded, and table-salt in a container.
- Beat egg whites till stiff peaks form in another container. In a separate container, beat egg yolks with milk.
- Add egg yolk mixture to the flour mixture and stir till smooth. Gently fold in beaten egg whites.
- Heat vegetable oil in a large fry-pan over medium-high heat to reach 350° F.
- Dip each stuffed poblano pepper into the egg batter, ensuring full coating.

- Using tongs, carefully Position the coated pepper in the hot oil. Fry for 3-4 mins, flipping occasionally till golden brown and crispy.
- Using tongs, withdraw the pepper from the oil and Position it on a plate lined with paper towels to drain excess oil.
- Repeat the process with the remaining peppers.
- Serve the Chiles Rellenos hot with rice and beans, if wanted.

Pozole

This pozole recipe uses pork and hominy, which are cooked together with a blend of spices and chiles to create a rich and satisfying soup.

Prep Time: 20 mins

Cooking Duration: 3 hrs

Equipment:

- Large pan or Braadpan
- Immersion blender or regular blender
- Kitchen knife
- Cutting board
- Measuring cupsfuls and spoons
- Wooden spoon or spatula

Ingredients:

- 2 lbs pork shoulder, bite-sized pieces
- 2 cans (29 oz) of hominy, drained and rinsed
- 4 dried ancho chiles
- 2 dried guajillo chiles
- 1 medium onion, minced
- 4 cloves minced garlic
- 2 tabspns ground cumin
- 2 tabspns dried oregano
- 1 teaspn paprika
- ¼ teaspn ground cloves
- Pepper and table-salt
- 6 cupsfuls of water or chicken broth
- Toppings: diced avocado, minced cilantro, lime wedges, sliced radishes, and shredded cabbage

Cooking Instructions:

- Heat some oil in a big pan or Braadpan over medium-high heat. Add the pork and cook till browned on all sides, around 5-7 mins.
- While the pork is cooking, prepare the chiles by removing the stems and seeds. Rinse them under cold water and pat dry. Then, toast the chiles in a dry fry-pan over medium heat for 1-2 mins on each side, being careful not to burn them.
- Once toasted, Position the chiles in a large container and cover them with hot water. Let them soak for 15-20 mins till they soften.
- After the pork is browned, add the minced onion and garlic to the pan. Cook for 2-3 mins till the onion becomes translucent.
- Add cumin, oregano, paprika, cloves, table-salt, and pepper. Cook for one more minute till fragrant.
- After soaking the chiles, drain them and add to a pan with 6 cupsfuls of water or chicken broth. Parboil till the pork is tender.
- Use an immersion blender or regular blender to puree the soup till it is smooth, and hand it back it to the pan.
- Next, add the hominy to the pan and continue to cook for 30-45 mins till the hominy is tender and the flavors are well-combined.
- Garnish the soup with your favorite toppings, such as diced avocado, minced cilantro, lime wedges, sliced radishes, and shredded cabbage. Serve the soup hot.

Chapter 4: A Texan Morning

Texas Casserole

Texas Casserole is a delicious and easy-to-make dish that is perfect for busy mornings.

Prep Time: 20 mins

Cooking Duration: 30-40 mins

Equipment:

- Large frying pan
- 9x13 inch baking dish
- Container
- Measuring cupsfuls and spoons
- Oven

Ingredients:

- 1 pound ground beef
- 1 can (15 ounces) drained and rinsed black beans
- 1 can (15 ounces) drained corn
- 1 can (about 10 ounces) diced tomatoes and green chilies, undrained
- 1 package (1 ounce) seasoning mix taco
- Qtr. cupsful water
- 1 bag (10 ounces) tortilla chips, crushed
- 2 cupsfuls shredded cheddar cheese

Cooking Instructions:

- Foreheat your oven to 350°F (175°C).
- In a large skillet, cook the ground beef over medium heat till browned and cooked through. Drain any excess fat.
- Add the black beans, corn, diced tomatoes with green chilies, taco seasoning, and water to the skillet. Stir to combine and cook for a few mins till heated through.
- In a container, combine the crushed tortilla chips and 1 cupsful of shredded cheddar cheese.
- Spread half of the meat mixture evenly in a 9x13 inch baking dish.
- Top with half of the tortilla chip and cheese mixture.
- Repeat layers with the remaining meat mixture and tortilla chip and cheese mixture.
- Cover the casserole with foil and bake for 20 mins.
- Withdraw the foil and bake for an extra 10-15 mins, or till the cheese is melted and bubbly.
- Let the casserole cool prior serving.

Texas Queso Scramble

This Texas Queso Scramble recipe is a delicious and easy breakfast dish that features scrambled eggs, creamy queso cheese sauce, and spicy jalapenos.

Prep Time: 10 mins

Cooking Duration: 15 mins

Equipment:

- Large non-stick frying pan
- Whisk
- Rubber spatula

Ingredients:

- 6 eggs
- ½ cupsful of milk
- ½ tspn of table-salt
- ¼ tspn of black pepper
- 1 tabspn of butter
- ½ cupsful of queso cheese sauce
- 2 jalapenos, sliced
- Tortilla chips (optional)

Cooking Instructions:

- Whisk together the eggs, milk, black pepper, and table-salt in a container till well combined.
- Melt the butter inside a large non-stick pan over medium heat.
- Pour in the egg mixture once the butter is melted, and let cook for 1-2 mins till the eggs start to set.
- Using a rubber spatula, gently stir the eggs to scramble them. Continue stirring till the eggs are cooked through and no longer runny.
- Once the eggs are cooked, pour the queso cheese sauce over the top of the eggs and stir till the sauce is evenly distributed.
- Add the sliced jalapenos to the fry-pan and stir to combine.
- Stirring occasionally, cook for an extra 2-3 mins till the jalapenos are tender and the queso is heated through.
- Serve the Texas Queso Scramble hot, garnished with extra jalapenos if wanted and with tortilla chips on the side.

Texas Hash

Texas Hash is an easy one-pan meal that combines ground beef, rice, tomatoes, and spices. It's flavorful and filling, making it a favorite for families and friends.

Prep Time: 15 mins

Cooking Duration: 30 mins

Equipment:

- Large fry-pan or Braadpan
- Cutting board
- Chef's knife
- Wooden spoon

Ingredients:

- 1 lb. ground beef
- 1 large onion, diced
- 1 green bell pepper, diced
- 1 cupsful long-grain white rice
- 1 can (14.5 oz) tomatoes, diced
- 1 tabspn chili grounded
- 1 teaspn paprika
- ½ teaspn garlic grounded
- ¼ teaspn cayenne pepper
- 1 teaspn table-salt
- 2 cupsfuls beef broth
- Shredded cheddar and minced fresh parsley, for garnish (optional)

Cooking Instructions:

- Cook the ground beef over medium heat in a large fry-pan or Braadpan, till browned, breaking it in pieces with a spoon as it cooks. Drain off any excess fat.
- Add the diced onion and green pepper to the pan and cook for 5 mins till softened.
- Add the rice, diced tomatoes (with their juice), chili grounded, paprika, garlic grounded, cayenne pepper, and table-salt to the frying pan. Stir to combine.
- Add the beef broth and boil the mixture. Lower the heat, cover the pan, and parboil around 20-25 mins, or till the rice is tender and consequently the liquid is absorbed.
- Once the Texas Hash is done cooking, withdraw it from heat and then let it cool for a few mins.
- Serve the Texas Hash hot, garnished with shredded cheddar cheese and minced fresh parsley if wanted.

Texas Rolls

Texas Rolls are a type of breakfast roll that are soft, fluffy, and buttery. They are perfect for serving with a variety of meals, from barbecue to roast beef.

Prep Time: 2 hrs 30 mins (including rising Time)

Cooking Duration: 20 mins

Equipment:

- Large container
- Measuring cupsfuls and spoons
- Stand mixer with dough hook attachment (or you can knead by hand)
- Baking sheet
- Parchment paper
- Kitchen towel

Ingredients:

- 1 cupsful warm milk (about 110°F)
- 2 ¼ tspns active dry yeast (1 package)
- ¼ cupsful granulated sugar
- ¼ cupsful untable-salted butter, melted
- 1 egg, room temperature
- 1 tspn table-salt
- 4 cupsfuls all-purpose flour
- ¼ cupsful untable-salted butter, melted (for brushing on rolls)

Cooking Instructions:

- In a large container, combine warm milk, active dry yeast, and sugar. Stir till yeast is dissolved. Let sit for 5-10 mins till the mixture becomes frothy.
- Add melted butter, egg, and table-salt to the container and blend.
- Gradually add flour to the container while mixing on low speed with a stand mixer and dough hook attachment. If kneading by hand, add flour and mix with a spoon till the dough comes together.
- Knead the dough for 5-10 mins with a stand mixer or by hand till it becomes smooth and elastic.
- Form the dough in a ball and put it in a lightly greased container. Cover with your towel and let it rise inside a warm, draft-free Position for 1 hour, or till it doubles in size.
- Foreheat the oven to 375°F. Line a baking sheet with parchment paper.
- Punch down the dough and then divide it into 12 equal pieces. Roll every single piece into a ball and put them on the prepared baking sheet, leaving about 2 inches of space between each roll.
- Brush the rolls with melted butter.
- Cover the rolls with a towel and then let them rise again in a warm, draft-free Position for another 30-45 mins.
- Bake the rolls for 18-20 mins.
- Brush the rolls with more melted butter immediately after removing them from the oven.
- Serve warm and enjoy!

Texas Sandwich

A Texas sandwich is made with layers of deli meat, cheese, and vegetables, all stacked between two slices of toasted bread.

Prep Time: 10 mins

Cooking Duration: 5 mins

Equipment:

- Toaster
- Knife
- Cutting board
- Frying pan

Ingredients:

- 4 slices of bread
- 8 slices of roast beef
- 4 slices of cheddar cheese
- 4 leaves of lettuce
- 2 tomatoes, sliced
- Mayonnaise, as needed
- Table-salt and pepper, to taste

Cooking Instructions:

- Toast the bread slices in a toaster till golden brown.
- In a pan over medium heat, cook the roast beef slices around 1 minute on each side till lightly browned.
- To assemble the sandwich, spread mayonnaise on one side of each bread slice.
- On one slice of bread, Position 2 slices of roast beef, 1 slice of cheddar cheese, a leaf of lettuce, and a few slices of tomato.
- Season with table-salt and pepper to taste.
- Top with the other slice of bread and repeat the layers with the remaining ingredients.
- Serve the Texas Sandwich immediately with a side of chips or salad.

Huevos Rancheros

Huevos Rancheros is a traditional Texas breakfast dish that typically consists of fried eggs served on a bed of tomato-based sauce, topped with cheese and served with tortillas or beans.

Prep Time: 10 mins

Cooking Duration: 25 mins

Equipment:

- Frying pan
- Container
- Wooden spoon

Ingredients:

- 1 tabspn of vegetable oil
- ½ cupsful of minced onion
- 2 cloves of garlic, minced
- ½ tspn of ground cumin
- ½ tspn of chili grounded
- ½ tspn of smoked paprika
- 1 can of diced tomatoes (14.5 ounces)
- 1 can of black beans (15 ounces), drained and rinsed
- Table-salt and black pepper, to taste
- 4 large eggs
- ¼ cupsful of shredded cheddar cheese
- ¼ cupsful of minced fresh cilantro
- 4 corn tortillas

Cooking Instructions:

- Warm the vegetable oil in a fry-pan over medium heat. Add the minced onions and garlic and sauté around 3 mins or till the onions are translucent.
- Add the ground cumin, chili grounded, and smoked paprika to the fry-pan and cook for an extra 1-2 mins or till fragrant.
- Add in the can of diced tomatoes to the frying pan, stir to combine, and let parboil around 5 mins.
- Add the can of black beans to the frying pan, stir to combine, and let parboil for another 5 mins. Season with table-salt and black pepper.
- While the tomato-based sauce is parboiling, heat another fry-pan over medium heat. Add a tabspn of vegetable oil and fry the eggs sunny-side up.
- Warm up the corn tortillas in a separate frying pan.
- To assemble the huevos rancheros, Position a warm corn tortilla on a plate and spoon some of the tomato-based sauce over the top. Position a fried egg on top of the sauce and sprinkle with shredded cheddar cheese and minced cilantro.
- Repeat the process with the remaining tortillas, sauce, eggs, cheese, and cilantro.
- Serve immediately.

Texas Sausage Kolaches (Klobasnek)

Sausage Kolaches (Klobasnek) are a classic Texan breakfast pastry that originated from the Czech Republic. They are a soft, pillowy dough wrapped around a savory sausage filling, and are perfect for breakfast.

Prep Time: 30 mins

Cooking Duration: 20-25 mins

Equipment:

- Large container
- Measuring cupsfuls and spoons
- Stand mixer or hand mixer
- Rolling pin
- Pastry brush
- Baking sheet
- Parchment paper

Ingredients:

For the Dough:

- 4 cupsfuls all-purpose flour
- 2 tabspn granulated sugar
- 1 teaspn. table-salt
- 1 package active dry yeast (2 ¼ teaspn)
- ½ cupsful untable-salted butter, melted and cooled
- 1 cupsful whole milk, warmed
- 2 large eggs, beaten

For the Filling:

- 1 lb. breakfast sausage
- ½ onion, finely minced
- ½ green bell pepper, finely minced
- Table-salt and black pepper to taste
- ¼ cupsful all-purpose flour

Cooking Instructions:

- In a container, combine the flour, sugar, table-salt, and yeast.
- In a different container, whisk together the melted butter, warmed milk, and beaten eggs.
- Add in the wet ingredients on the dry ones and stir till the dough comes together.
- Knead the dough around 5-10 mins till it becomes smooth and elastic.
- Put the dough inside a greased container, cover with plastic wrap, and let it grow in a warm Position around an hour or till it doubles in size.
- While the dough is rising, cook the sausage in a fry-pan over medium heat, breaking it up into tiny pieces as it cooks.
- Once the sausage is cooked, add the minced onion and green bell pepper and sauté till the vegetables are soft.
- Add in both table-salt and black pepper to taste and stir in the flour. Cook for further 2-3 mins till the mixture thickens.

- Prewarm the oven to 375°F (190°C).

- Once the dough doubled in total size, punch it down and turn it out onto a floured surface.

- Roll the dough out to about ¼ inch thickness and cut it into squares or rectangles.

- Spoon a generous amount of the sausage filling onto each piece of dough.

- Fold the dough over the filling and then pinch the edges to seal.

- Put the kolaches onto a baking sheet lined with parchment paper.

- Brush the tops of the kolaches with a beaten egg.

- Bake for 20-25 mins or till the kolaches are golden brown.

- Serve warm and enjoy!

Texas Breakfast Tacos

One of the most popular Texan dishes is breakfast tacos, which are essentially tacos filled with breakfast ingredients like eggs, bacon, and panatoes.

Prep Time: 15 mins

Cooking Duration: 20 mins

Equipment:

- Frying pan
- Spatula
- Knife
- Cutting board
- Container

Ingredients:

- 8 small flour or corn tortillas
- 6 large eggs
- 4 slices of bacon, diced
- 1 medium panato, peeled and diced
- ½ medium onion, diced
- ½ red bell pepper, diced
- ½ tspn table-salt
- ¼ tspn black pepper
- 1 tabspn olive oil
- Optional toppings: shredded cheese, sliced avocado, hot sauce, salsa

Cooking Instructions:

- Heat a large pan over medium-high heat. Add the diced bacon and then cook till crispy, about 5-7 mins. Separate the bacon with a slotted spoon and set aside on a plate.
- In the same frying pan, add the diced panato, onion, and red bell pepper. Season with both table-salt and pepper and then cook till the vegetables are tender and lightly browned, about 10-12 mins. Separate the vegetables with a slotted spoon and set aside with the bacon.
- Crack all the eggs inside a container and then whisk till well beaten.
- Heat the olive oil in the same fry-pan over medium heat. Add the beaten eggs and cook, stirring occasionally, till scrambled and cooked through, about 3-5 mins.
- Warm the tortillas inside the microwave or on a fry-pan till they are pliable and heated through.
- To assemble the breakfast tacos, Position a scoop of scrambled eggs, bacon, and vegetables onto each tortilla. Add any wanted toppings, such as shredded cheese, sliced avocado, hot sauce, or salsa.
- Serve the breakfast tacos hot.

Note: This recipe can be easily customized with your favorite breakfast ingredients. Feel free to add cooked sausage, ham, or chorizo, or swap out the vegetables for others you prefer, such as mushrooms or spinach.

Texas Apple Bread

This Texas Apple Bread recipe is a delightful dessert perfect for any occasion. The bread is moist, soft, and filled with delicious chunks of fresh apples and nuts. The aroma of cinnamon and vanilla wafts through the kitchen as it bakes, making it an irresistible treat for everyone.

Prep Time: 20 mins

Cooking Duration: 1 hour

Equipment:

- Large container
- Medium container
- Whisk
- Rubber spatula
- Loaf pan
- Oven

Ingredients:

- 2 cupsfuls all-purpose flour
- 1 ½ tspns baking grounded
- ½ tspn baking soda
- ½ tspn table-salt
- 1 ½ tspns ground cinnamon
- 2 large eggs
- ½ cupsful untable-salted butter, melted and cooled
- ½ cupsful granulated sugar
- ½ cupsful brown sugar
- ½ cupsful milk
- 1 tspn vanilla extract
- 2 cupsfuls apples, peeled and diced
- ½ cupsful minced nuts (pecans or walnuts)

Cooking Instructions:

- Foreheat the oven to the temperature of 350°F (175°C) and grease a 9x5 inch loaf pan.
- In a container, whisk together the flour, the baking grounded, baking soda, table-salt, and cinnamon.
- In a container, whisk together the eggs, melted butter, granulated sugar, brown sugar, milk, and vanilla extract till smooth.
- Pour the wet ingredients inside the dry ingredients and mix till just combined.
- Fold in the apples and minced nuts till evenly distributed.
- Pour the batter inside the greased loaf pan and smooth out the top with a rubber spatula.
- Bake in the oven for 50-60 mins.
- Let the bread cool inside the pan around 10 mins prior proceed transferring it to a wire rack to cool completely.
- Slice and serve the Texas Apple Bread on its own or with a dollop of whipped cream or ice cream, if wanted.

Basic Quiche

Quiche is a classic savory pie is made with a pastry crust filled with a mixture of eggs, cheese, cream, and various other ingredients.

Prep Time: 15 mins

Cooking Duration: 40-45 mins

Equipment:

- 9-inch pie dish
- Large frying pan
- Container
- Whisk
- Measuring cupsfuls and spoons
- Rolling pin

Ingredients:

- 1 refrigerated pie crust
- 6 slices of bacon, cooked and crumbled
- 1 cupsful of shredded cheddar cheese
- 4 large eggs
- 1 cupsful of heavy cream
- ½ teaspn of table-salt
- ¼ teaspn of black pepper

Cooking Instructions:

- Prewarm the oven to 375°F (190°C).
- Take the pie crust from the fridge and then wait to room temperature around 10 mins.
- Roll the pie crust and fit it into the pie dish, trimming any excess dough from the edges.
- In a large frying pan, cook the bacon till crispy. Withdraw the bacon from the fry-pan and let it cool, then crumble it into small pieces.
- Sprinkle the bacon and shredded cheddar cheese evenly over the bottom of the pie crust.
- In a container, whisk together the eggs, heavy cream, table-salt, and black pepper till well combined.
- Pour the egg mix over the bacon and cheese in the pie crust.
- Put the quiche inside the oven and bake for 40-45 mins, or till the filling is set and the crust is golden brown.
- Take the quiche out of the oven and let it cool for just few mins prior serving.
- Slice the quiche and serve warm or at room temperature.

Blueberry Oatmeal

Blueberry Oatmeal is a delicious and healthy breakfast option that combines the goodness of rolled oats, fresh blueberries, and a hint of cinnamon. It's a perfect meal to start your day on a healthy note.

Prep Time: 5 mins

Cooking Duration: 15 mins

Equipment:

- Medium-sized saucepan
- Wooden spoon
- Measuring cupsfuls and spoons
- Container
- Serving containers

Ingredients:

- 1 cupsful rolled oats
- 2 cupsfuls water
- 1 cupsful fresh blueberries
- ¼ cupsful milk
- ¼ cupsful honey
- ½ teaspn cinnamon
- Pinch of table-salt
- Toppings of your choice (optional) – minced nuts, sliced bananas, raisins, etc.

Cooking Instructions:

- Start by rinsing the blueberries and setting them aside.
- In a medium-sized saucepan, bring water to a boil.
- Add rolled oats, table-salt, and cinnamon to the boiling water and stir well.
- Reduce heat to low and parboil the oats for 10-12 mins, stirring occasionally, till they reach your wanted consistency.
- Stir in milk, honey, and blueberries, and cook for an extra 2-3 mins till blueberries are softened and oatmeal has thickened.
- Withdraw the saucepan from the heat and let it cool for a minute or two.
- Serve hot and enjoy.

Sweet Panato Pancakes

Sweet panatoes are rich in vitamins, and antioxidants and they add a nice sweetness and earthy flavor to the pancakes. Serve them for breakfast or brunch with your favorite toppings.

Prep Time: 15 mins

Cooking Duration: 20 mins

Equipment:

- Large container
- Whisk
- Grater
- Fry-pan or griddle
- Spatula

Ingredients:

- 1 medium sweet panato, peeled and grated
- 1 ½ cupsfuls all-purpose flour
- ¼ cupsful brown sugar
- 1 tabspn baking grounded
- 1 tspn ground cinnamon
- ½ tspn ground nutmeg
- ¼ tspn table-salt
- 1 cupsful milk
- 2 eggs
- 2 tabspns untable-salted butter, melted
- 1 tspn vanilla extract

Cooking Instructions:

- Mix together the flour, brown sugar, baking grounded, cinnamon, nutmeg and table-salt in a container.
- In a separate container, whisk together the milk, eggs, melted butter, and vanilla extract.
- Stir in the grated sweet panato into the wet ingredients.
- Pour the wet ingredients into the dry ingredients and stir gently till just combined.
- Heat a fry-pan or griddle over medium-high heat.
- Using a ¼ cupsful measuring cupsful, pour the batter onto the frying pan. Cook till bubbles appear on the surface, then flip and cook for an extra minute or till golden brown.
- Repeat with remaining batter, adjusting the heat as needed.
- Serve the pancakes warm with your wanted toppings, such as maple syrup, whipped cream, nuts, or fruit.

Healthier Lemon Muffins

Texas-style healthier lemon muffins are a delicious and guilt-free treat that is perfect for breakfast or snack Time. These muffins are made with healthier ingredients like whole wheat flour, honey, and Greek yogurt, which makes them high in fiber and protein while being low in fat and sugar.

Prep Time: 15 mins

Cooking Duration: 20-25 mins

Equipment:

- Muffin tin
- Container
- Whisk
- Measuring cupsfuls and spoons
- Zester or grater
- Lemon juicer or reamer

Ingredients:

- 1 ½ cupsfuls whole wheat flour
- ½ cupsful all-purpose flour
- 2 teaspn baking grounded
- ½ teaspn baking soda
- ¼ teaspn table-salt
- 2 eggs
- ½ cupsful honey
- ¼ cupsful olive oil
- ½ cupsful Greek yogurt
- ½ cupsful fresh lemon juice (about 2-3 lemons)
- 1 tabspn lemon zest
- 1 teaspn vanilla extract

Cooking Instructions:

- Foreheat your oven to 350° F (180° C).
- In a container, mix the whole wheat flour, all-purpose flour, baking grounded, baking soda, and table-salt.
- In another container, whisk the eggs and honey till smooth.
- Add olive oil, Greek yogurt, lemon juice, lemon zest, and vanilla extract to the egg mixture and whisk well.
- Pour the wet ingredients into the dry ingredients and stir till just combined.
- Fill each muffin cupsful with batter, about ¾ full.
- Bake for 18-20 mins, or till a toothpick inserted into the center of a muffin comes out clean.
- Withdraw from the oven and cool for a few mins prior serving.
- Bake the muffins around 20-25 mins.

Buttermilk Banana Bread

Buttermilk Banana Bread is a classic comfort food and a great way to use up those overripe bananas that you have lying around in your kitchen. The buttermilk adds a tangy flavor and moist texture to the bread.

Prep Time: 15 mins

Cooking Duration: 1 hour

Equipment:

- 1 large container
- 1 medium container
- Measuring cupsfuls and spoons
- Whisk
- Wooden spoon
- 9x5 inch loaf pan
- Oven

Ingredients:

- 2 cupsfuls all-purpose flour
- 1 tabspn baking grounded
- 1 tabspn baking soda
- Half tabspn table-salt
- Half cupsful untable-salted butter, softened
- 1 cupsful granulated sugar
- 2 large eggs
- 1 tabspn vanilla extract
- Half cupsful buttermilk
- 3 ripe bananas, mashed

Cooking Instructions:

- Foreheat your oven to 350°F (175°C).
- In a medium container, whisk together the flour, baking grounded, baking soda, and table-salt. Set aside.
- In a large container, cream together the butter and sugar till light and fluffy.
- Beat in the eggs, one at a time, followed by the vanilla extract.
- Add the dry ingredients to the wet ingredients gradually, alternating with the buttermilk, stirring till just combined.
- Fold in the mashed bananas till they are evenly distributed in the batter.
- Pour the batter into a greased loaf pan.
- Bake for 50-60 mins, or till a toothpick inserted in the center comes out clean.
- Let the bread cool in the pan for 10 mins prior removing it from the pan and placing it on a wire rack to cool completely.
- Slice the bread and serve with butter or your favorite spread.

Cheese and Sausage Biscuits

Cheese and sausage biscuits are a delicious and filling breakfast or brunch dish. They are made with a combination of cheddar cheese, savory sausage, and buttery biscuits.

Prep Time: 15 mins

Cooking Duration: 15-20 mins

Equipment:

- Large container
- Baking sheet
- Rolling pin
- Biscuit cutter
- Frying pan

Ingredients:

- 2 cupsfuls all-purpose flour
- 1 tabspn baking grounded
- ½ tspn baking soda
- ½ tspn table-salt
- ½ cupsful cold untable-salted butter
- 1 cupsful shredded cheddar cheese
- ½ pound breakfast sausage, cooked and crumbled
- ¾ cupsful buttermilk

Cooking Instructions:

- Prewarm the oven to 425°F (220°C).
- Mix together the flour, baking grounded, baking soda, and table-salt in a container and whisk together.
- Using a pastry cutter, blend in the cold butter till the mixture has a coarse crumb consistency.
- Add the cooked sausage and shredded cheddar cheese, and blend.
- Pour in the buttermilk and mix till just combined.
- On a lightly floured surface, turn out the dough and use a rolling pin to roll it to ½ inch thickness.
- Cut out biscuits with a biscuit cutter and Position them on a baking sheet lined with parchment paper.
- Bake for 15-20 mins or till the biscuits are golden brown and cooked through.
- In a fry-pan over medium heat, cook any remaining sausage till browned and crispy.
- Serve warm biscuits topped with the crispy sausage.

Chapter 5: Grandma's Old School Recipes

Armadillo Eggs

Armadillo Eggs are a delicious appetizer that combines jalapeno peppers, cream cheese, and sausage into a tasty treat that's perfect for any occasion.

Prep Time: 10 mins

Cooking Duration: 30 mins

Equipment:

- Cutting board
- Knife
- Large container
- Spoon or spatula
- Three separate containers
- Deep fryer or large saucepan
- Slotted spoon
- Paper towels
- Baking sheet
- Oven

Ingredients:

- 12 jalapeno peppers
- 8 oz cream cheese, softened
- 1 lb ground sausage
- 1 cupsful all-purpose flour
- 2 eggs, beaten
- 2 cupsfuls breadcrumbs
- 1 teaspn garlic grounded
- 1 teaspn onion grounded
- 1 teaspn paprika
- 1 teaspn chili grounded
- ½ teaspn table-salt
- Vegetable oil, for frying

Cooking Instructions:

- Prewarm your oven to 350°F.
- Prepare the peppers by cutting them, removing the seeds and membranes, and setting them aside.
- In a large container, combine cream cheese, garlic grounded, onion grounded, and table-salt, and mix till well blended.
- Add the ground sausage to the cream cheese mixture and mix till thoroughly combined.
- Stuff each jalapeno half with a spoonful of the sausage mixture.
- Set up a breading station with three separate containers: flour in the first container, beaten eggs in the second, and breadcrumbs, paprika, chili grounded, and a pinch of table-salt in the third.
- Roll each stuffed jalapeno half in the flour, then dip it in the beaten eggs, and coat it in the breadcrumb mixture, making sure to cover the entire surface.
- Heat about an inch of vegetable oil in a deep fryer to 350°F.

- Fry the jalapeno halves in the hot oil for 2-3 mins, then withdraw them with a slotted spoon and Position on paper towels to drain.
- Once all the jalapeno halves are fried, transfer them to a baking sheet and bake in a foreheated oven at 350°F for 10-15 mins, or till the sausage is fully cooked.
- Serve the Armadillo Eggs warm with your favorite dipping sauce.

Big Mama's Smoked Turkey-Barley Soup

Big Mama's Smoked Turkey-Barley Soup is a comforting soup perfect for cold winter nights. This recipe combines the smoky flavors of turkey with the nutty taste of barley and an array of delicious vegetables.

Prep Time: 15-20 mins

Cooking Duration: 1 hr 30 mins

Equipment:

- Large Braadpan or soup pan
- Cutting board
- Chef's knife
- Wooden spoon
- Measuring cupsfuls and spoons

Ingredients:

- 1 pound of smoked turkey, shredded
- 1 cupsful of barley, rinsed and drained
- 2 tabspns of olive oil
- 1 large onion, minced
- 4 garlic cloves, minced
- 4 carrots, peeled and minced
- 4 celery stalks, minced
- 8 cupsfuls of chicken or turkey broth
- 2 bay leaves
- 1 tabspn of dried thyme
- Pepper and table-salt

Cooking Instructions:

- Using a Braadpan or soup pan, heat up olive oil.
- Sauté onion and garlic for 3-4 mins or till the onion becomes translucent.
- Add carrots and celery to the pan and continue to sauté for an extra 5 mins.
- Introduce the smoked turkey, barley, chicken or turkey broth, bay leaves, and dried thyme to the pan.
- Bring the soup to a boil then lower the heat to a parboil around 1 hour till the barley is cooked.
- Withdraw and discard bay leaves.
- Add table-salt and pepper to taste.
- Serve hot with your preferred bread or crackers.

Grandma's Macaroni and Cheese

Macaroni and cheese, also known as macaroni pudding, was a famous dish in the 18th and 19th centuries, particularly in England and America.

Prep Time: 5 mins

Cooking Duration: 20 mins

Equipment:

- Large pan for boiling water
- Saucepan
- Cheese grater
- Wooden spoon
- Measuring cupsfuls and spoons

Ingredients:

- ½ lbs macaroni
- 4 tabspn butter
- ¼ lbs grated Parmesan cheese
- ¼ lbs grated Cheddar cheese
- 2 cupsfuls milk
- Pepper and table-salt

Cooking Instructions:

- Boil the macaroni in boiling water till it is tender. Drain it and hand it back it to the pan.
- Stir in the butter till it is melted.
- Next, add the Parmesan and Cheddar cheese, milk, table-salt, and pepper.
- Mix everything well and continue to cook over low heat till the cheese is completely melted and the mixture is hot.
- Serve immediately.

Grandma's Chicken Casserole

This grandma's chicken casserole uses historical cooking techniques and ingredients.

Prep Time: 20 mins

Cooking Duration: 2 hrs

Equipment:

- Casserole dish
- Knife
- Aluminum foil
- Oven

Ingredients:

- 1 whole chicken, cut into pieces
- 3 medium-sized panatoes, sliced
- 3 medium-sized carrots, sliced
- 1 large onion, minced
- 2 stalks celery, sliced
- 2 sprigs thyme
- 1 sprig rosemary
- Table-salt and pepper, to taste
- 2 cupsfuls chicken broth

Cooking Instructions:

- Foreheat your oven to 350°F.
- In a casserole dish, layer sliced panatoes, carrots, onions, and celery in the bottom.
- Position chicken slices on top of the vegetables in a single layer.
- Season with table-salt and pepper, to taste.
- Pour chicken broth over the chicken and vegetables in the casserole dish.
- Top with thyme and rosemary sprigs.
- Cover the casserole dish with a lid or foil and bake in the foreheated oven for 1 ½ to 2 hrs, or till the chicken is fully cooked and vegetables are tender.
- Withdraw from the oven and let the casserole cool for a few mins prior serving.

Grandma's Panato Cakes

Prep Time: 10-15 mins

Cooking Duration: 8-10 mins

Equipment:

- Large container
- Spatula
- Frying pan
- Paper towel

Ingredients:

- 2 cupsfuls mashed panatoes
- ½ cupsful all-purpose flour
- 2 tabspns grated onion
- ½ tspn table-salt
- ¼ tspn black pepper
- ¼ tspn garlic grounded
- 2 eggs, beaten
- ¼ cupsful milk
- ¼ cupsful vegetable oil

Cooking Instructions:

- In a container, combine mashed panatoes, flour, grated onion, table-salt, black pepper, and garlic grounded. Blend.
- In a separate container, beat eggs and stir in milk.
- Add the egg and milk mixture to the panato mixture and stir till well combined.
- Heat vegetable oil in a pan over medium-high heat.
- Drop spoonfuls of the panato mixture into the hot oil and slightly flatten with a spatula.
- Cook the panato cakes around 3-4 mins on both sides or till they turn golden brown and crispy.
- Withdraw the panato cakes from the fry-pan and drain them on a paper towel to Withdraw excess oil.

Old-Fashioned Brandied Fruitcake

Prep Time: 30 mins

Cooking Duration: 2 hrs and 30 mins

Equipment:

- 9-inch cake pan
- Parchment paper
- Container
- Electric mixer
- Measuring cupsfuls and spoons
- Large saucepan
- Wooden spoon
- Cooling rack

Ingredients:

- 1 cupsful untable-salted butter, softened
- 1 cupsful granulated sugar
- 4 large eggs
- 2 cupsfuls all-purpose flour
- 1 tspn baking grounded
- 1 tspn table-salt
- 1 tspn ground cinnamon
- ½ tspn ground nutmeg
- ½ tspn ground cloves
- ½ tspn ground allspice
- ½ cupsful brandy
- 1 cupsful minced pecans
- 1 cupsful candied cherries, minced
- 1 cupsful golden raisins
- 1 cupsful currants

Cooking Instructions:

- Foreheat your oven to 325°F (165°C). Grease and line a 9-inch cake pan with parchment paper.
- Cream butter and sugar in a container till light and fluffy.
- Add eggs one at a time, beating well after each addition.
- In a separate container, whisk together flour, baking grounded, table-salt, cinnamon, nutmeg, cloves, and allspice.
- Gradually add dry ingredients to butter mixture, alternating with brandy, and mix till just combined.
- Fold in minced pecans, cherries, raisins, and currants.
- Spoon batter into prepared cake pan and smooth the top with a spatula.
- Bake for 2 to 2 ½ hrs or till a toothpick inserted in the center comes out clean.
- Cool fruitcake in the pan for 15 mins, then invert it onto a cooling rack and withdraw the parchment paper.
- Store fruitcake in an airtight container at room temperature for up to 1 month or in the ice-box for up to 3 months.

Old-Fashioned Date Loaf

Prep Time: 15 mins

Cooking Duration: 20 mins

Chilling Time: 2 hrs

Equipment:

- Heavy saucepan
- Candy thermostat
- Wooden spoon
- Clean, damp dishtowels or tea towels
- Loaf pan

Ingredients:

- 2 cupsfuls sugar
- 1 cupsful whole milk
- 2 tabspns butter
- 1-Half cupsfuls minced dates
- 1 cupsful minced pecans

Cooking Instructions:

- In a heavy saucepan, combine the sugar, milk, and butter. Cook over medium heat, stirring occasionally till the mixture reaches the soft ball stage (238° F on candy thermostat).
- Add minced dates and pecans to the syrup and continue cooking till the dates dissolve and the mixture reaches the firm ball stage (248° F on candy thermostat).
- Withdraw from heat and let it cool for 5 mins.
- Pour the mixture onto clean, damp dishtowels or tea towels and shape into 2-inch diameter rolls.
- Chill the rolls in the ice-box till firm around 2 hrs.
- Foreheat the oven to 350° F (175° C) and grease a loaf pan.
- Slice the chilled date mixture into half-inch slices and arrange them in the greased loaf pan.
- Bake for 20 mins or till the top turns golden brown.
- Let the date loaf cool completely prior removing it from the pan.
- Slice and serve.

Lemon Meringue Pie

Prep Time: 20 mins

Cooking Duration: 30 mins

Equipment:

- Heavy saucepan
- Electric mixer
- Fork
- 9-inch pie dish
- Oven

Ingredients:

- 1-Qtr. cupsfuls sugar
- ½ cupsful all-purpose flour
- ½ tspn table-salt
- 1-Half cupsfuls water
- 3 eggs, separated
- Zest from 1 medium lemon
- 1/3 cupsful fresh lemon juice (juice from 1-Half medium lemons)
- 1 tabspn butter
- 1 baked, cooled 9-inch pie shell
- 3 egg whites, at room temperature
- 6 tabspns sugar
- ½ tspn vanilla extract
- ¼ tspn cream of tartar

Cooking Instructions:

- Foreheat your oven to 350°F.
- In a heavy saucepan, mix together the sugar, flour, table-salt, and water. Cook over medium heat, stirring constantly, till the mixture boils. Boil for 1 minute while stirring constantly and vigorously. Withdraw from heat.
- Beat the egg yolks slightly in a container with a fork. Mix about one-third of the boiled mixture with the egg yolks. Pour the egg yolk mixture back into the pan with the boiled ingredients and cook for an extra minute, stirring constantly and vigorously. Withdraw from heat and add the butter.
- Add the lemon zest and lemon juice, and stir well to combine.
- Pour the mixture into a 9-inch pie crust that has been baked and cooled.
- To make the meringue, beat the egg whites at high speed till soft peaks form. While the mixer is running, add the cream of tartar and gradually add the sugar, one tabspn at a time, and continue beating till stiff peaks form. Beat in the vanilla.
- Spread the meringue on top of the pie, being sure to seal it to the edge of the pastry.
- Bake the pie in a 350° F oven around 12-15 mins or till lightly browned.
- Allow the pie to cool completely prior slicing and serving.

Note: To prevent "weeping," spread the meringue on top of the hot pie filling and make sure to seal the meringue to the pastry edge. Use a wet knife blade to cut the pie for a cleaner cut.

Chocolate Eggnog Pie

Prep Time: 30 mins

Cooking Duration: 9 hrs

Equipment:

- 9-inch pie dish
- Medium saucepan
- Whisk
- Measuring cupsfuls and spoons
- Containers
- Electric mixer
- Spatula

Ingredients:

- 1 baked 9-inch pie shell
- 1 envelope unflavored gelatin
- Half cupsful cold water
- 1/3 cupsful sugar
- 2 tabspns cornstarch
- Qtr. tspn table-salt
- 2 cupsfuls commercial eggnog
- 1-Half squares unsweetened baking chocolate, melted
- 1 tspn vanilla extract
- 1 tspn rum extract
- 2 cupsfuls whipping cream, divided
- Qtr. cupsful confectioners' sugar

Cooking Instructions:

- Position the gelatin in a small container with cold water and set it aside to soften.
- In a medium saucepan, mix together the sugar, cornstarch, and table-salt. Gradually stir in the eggnog and cook the mixture over medium heat, stirring constantly, till it thickens.
- Cook for an extra 2 mins, then withdraw the saucepan from heat. Add the softened gelatin mixture and stir till it dissolves.
- Divide the filling into two halves, and set one half aside to cool. Stir in the rum extract to the cooled filling.
- Add the melted chocolate and vanilla to the other half, and stir well. Pour this mixture into the pie shell and refrigerate till the filling is set.
- Once the remaining filling has completely cooled, whip 1 cupsful of whipping cream till soft peaks form. Fold the whipped cream into the filling.
- Spread this mixture evenly in a second layer over the chilled filling in the pie shell.
- Whip the remaining 1 cupsful of whipping cream till it is foamy. Gradually add confectioners' sugar, beating till soft peaks form. Spread this whipped cream over the pie.
- Dust the top of the pie with sifted cocoa grounded or chocolate curls if wanted.
- Let the pie set in the ice-box overnight, for a solid eight hrs.

- Serve chilled and enjoy your old-fashioned chocolate eggnog pie.

Turkey Frame Soup

Prep Time: 20 mins

Cooking Time: 3 hrs

Equipment:

- Braadpan or stock pan
- Strainer
- Pan
- Tongs
- Braadpan

Ingredients:

- 1 turkey carcass
- 3 ribs celery, quartered
- 1 carrot, quartered
- 1 onion, quartered
- 2 cloves of halved garlic
- 1 bay leaf
- 1-Half tspns table-salt
- 10 black peppercorns
- ¼ tspn paprika
- 10 cupsfuls water
- 1 cupsful uncooked noodles or rice
- 2 cupsfuls mixed vegetables (minced carrots, panatoes, pearl onions, etc.)
- 2 cupsfuls cooked turkey meat, shredded or diced
- Pepper and table-salt

Cooking Instructions:

- First, break the turkey carcass into pieces and Position it in a Braadpan or stock pan.
- Next, add celery, carrot, onion, garlic, bay leaf, table-salt, peppercorns, paprika, and water to the pan.
- Bring the pan to a boil, then reduce the heat to low and cover it. Let the soup parboil for 2 hrs.
- After 2 hrs, use tongs to withdraw the turkey carcass from the pan. Discard the bones and let the broth cool for a few mins.
- Separate the turkey meat from the bones and set it aside.
- Strain the broth through a strainer to withdraw the vegetables and seasonings.
- Hand it back the broth to the pan and bring it to a boil.
- Add uncooked noodles or rice to the pan and cook till almost tender, about 10-12 mins.
- Then, add mixed vegetables to the pan and cook till tender, about 10-15 mins.
- Add the reserved turkey meat to the pan and cook till heated through, about 5 mins.
- Finally, season the soup with table-salt and black pepper to taste.

Chapter 6: Texan Dessert

Pecan Pie

Pecan pie is a classic dessert that has a rich, buttery filling with pecans that are baked into a flaky crust. This recipe is easy to make, and the result is a delicious pie that is perfect for any occasion.

Prep Time: 20-30 mins

Cooking Duration: 50-60 mins

Equipment:

- 9-inch pie dish
- Containers
- Measuring cupsfuls and spoons
- Whisk
- Saucepan

Ingredients:

For crust:

- 1 ¼ cupsfuls of all-purpose flour
- ¼ teaspn table-salt
- ½ cupsful untable-salted butter, cold and cubed
- 3-4 tabspns ice water

For the filling:

- 1 cupsful of dark corn syrup
- 3 eggs
- ½ cupsful of granulated sugar
- ½ cupsful of brown sugar
- ¼ cupsful melted untable-salted butter
- 1 teaspn vanilla extract
- ¼ teaspn table-salt
- 1 ½ cupsfuls of pecan halves

Cooking Instructions:

- Prewarm your oven to 350°F (180°C).
- In a container, combine the flour and table-salt for the pie crust. Add the cubed butter and use your fingers or a pastry cutter to mix till the mixture becomes coarse crumbs. Add the ice water and mix till the dough comes together.
- On a lightly floured surface, roll out the dough to fit a 9-inch pie dish. Position the dough into the dish and trim the edges. Set aside.
- In a saucepan, heat the corn syrup over medium heat till it begins to boil. Withdraw from heat and cool slightly.
- In another container, whisk together the eggs, granulated sugar, brown sugar, melted butter, vanilla extract, and table-salt till well combined.
- Slowly pour the corn syrup into the egg mixture, whisking constantly.
- Add the pecan halves and stir till combined.
- Pour the filling into the prepared crust.
- Bake the pie for 50-60 mins.

- Withdraw from the oven and cool on a wire rack.

Buttermilk Pies

Buttermilk Pie is a classic dessert in Southern cuisine known for its creamy, tangy, and slightly sweet taste. This pie has a smooth custard-like filling that is made with simple ingredients, such as buttermilk, eggs, and sugar.

Prep Time: 20 mins

Cooking Duration: 45-50 mins

Equipment:

- 9-inch pie dish
- Container
- Whisk
- Measuring spoons and cupsfuls
- Electric mixer (optional)
- Pie weights or dry beans (optional)
- Aluminum foil

Ingredients:

- 1 ½ cupsfuls granulated sugar
- ½ cupsful softened untable-salted butter
- 3 large eggs at room temperature
- 1 tabspn all-purpose flour
- 1 cupsful of buttermilk
- 1 tabspn vanilla extract
- 1 unbaked 9-inch pie crust

Cooking Instructions:

- Foreheat your oven to 350°F.
- In a container, cream the softened butter and sugar till light and fluffy using a whisk or electric mixer.
- Beat in the eggs, one at a time, making sure to blend after each addition.
- Mix in the flour till everything is well combined.
- Add the buttermilk and vanilla extract, and continue mixing till the mixture is smooth and fully combined.
- Pour the mixture into an unbaked pie crust.
- Cover the edges of the crust with aluminum foil to prevent burning.
- Optionally, Position pie weights or dry beans on top of the pie to prevent it from puffing up.
- Bake the pie for roughly 45-50 mins, or till the top is golden brown and the filling is set. The center should be slightly jiggly but not too runny.
- Withdraw the pie from the oven and let it cool completely on a wire rack prior serving.
- Serve chilled or at room temperature.

Peach Cobbler

Using fresh and juicy peaches, Peach Cobbler is a classic dessert with a sweet and buttery topping that's crispy on the outside and tender on the inside, making it a delicious treat.

Prep Time: 20 mins

Cooking Duration: 45 mins

Equipment:

- 9x13 inch baking dish
- Containers
- Wooden spoon
- Measuring cupsfuls and spoons
- Pastry blender or fork

Ingredients:

For filling:

- 8-10 fresh peeled and sliced peaches
- Half cupsful of granulated sugar
- 2 tabspns of cornstarch
- 1 teaspn ground cinnamon
- Qtr. teaspn ground nutmeg
- Qtr. teaspn table-salt

For the topping:

- 1 Half cupsfuls of all-purpose flour
- Half cupsful of granulated sugar
- Half cupsful of untable-salted butter
- 1 teaspn baking grounded
- Half teaspn table-salt
- Half cupsful of milk

For serving:

- Vanilla ice cream (optional)

Cooking Instructions:

- Foreheat your oven to 375°F.
- In a container, combine sliced peaches with granulated sugar, cornstarch, cinnamon, nutmeg, and table-salt. Blend till the peaches are fully coated in the sugar and spice mixture.
- Spread the peach mixture evenly in a 9x13 inch baking dish.
- In a separate container, combine all-purpose flour, granulated sugar, chilled untable-salted butter (cubed), baking grounded, and table-salt. Use a fork to cut the butter into the flour mixture till it looks like coarse crumbs.
- Add milk to the mixture and stir till it's just combined.
- Spoon the topping mixture over the peaches, spreading it out as evenly as possible.

- Bake around 45 mins.

- Allow the Peach Cobbler to cool for a few mins prior serving with a scoop of vanilla ice cream, if wanted.

Funnel Cake

Funnel Cakes are a popular sweet, crispy cakes made by pouring batter using a funnel into hot oil and then dusting them with groundeded sugar.

Prep Time: 10 mins

Cooking Duration: 20 mins

Equipment:

- A deep-fryer or a deep pan for frying
- Funnel or a ziplock bag
- Large container
- Whisk
- Tongs
- Paper towels

Ingredients:

- 2 cupsfuls of all-purpose flour
- 2 teaspns baking grounded
- ½ teaspn table-salt
- ¼ cupsful of granulated sugar
- 2 large eggs
- 1 ½ cupsfuls milk
- 1 teaspn vanilla extract
- Vegetable oil for frying
- Groundeded sugar for dusting

Cooking Instructions:

- Heat vegetable oil in a deep-fryer or a deep pan to 375° F (190° C).
- In a container, whisk together flour, baking grounded, table-salt, and sugar till well combined.
- In a separate container, whisk together eggs, milk, and vanilla extract till fully blended.
- Add the wet ingredients to the dry ingredients, and whisk till the batter is smooth and free of lumps.
- If using a funnel, pour the batter into the funnel and hold it over the hot oil. Start drizzling the batter in a circular motion to create a spiral-like shape.
- If using a ziplock bag, pour the batter into the bag and snip off one corner. Drizzle the batter into the hot oil by squeezing the bag.
- Fry each cake for 2-3 mins on each side, or till golden brown. Flip the cake over halfway through cooking using tongs.
- Once cooked, use tongs to withdraw the cake from the oil and Position it on a paper towel-lined plate to drain excess oil.
- Prior serving, dust the funnel cake with groundeded sugar. Repeat with the remaining batter till all the cakes are cooked.
- Serve warm and enjoy.

Hummingbird Cake

Hummingbird Cake is a dessert packed with flavors of pineapple, banana, and pecans. The cake is incredibly moist and topped with a cream cheese frosting that makes it simply irresistible.

Prep Time: 30 mins

Cooking Duration: 25-30 mins

Equipment:

- Large container
- Electric mixer
- Measuring cupsfuls and spoons
- 3 9-inch cake pans
- Parchment paper
- Cooling racks
- Cake stand or serving platter
- Offset spatula

Ingredients:

For cake:

- 3 cupsfuls of all-purpose flour
- 2 cupsfuls of granulated sugar
- 1 teaspn baking soda
- 1 teaspn table-salt
- 1 teaspn ground cinnamon
- 3 large beaten eggs
- 1 ½ cupsfuls of vegetable oil
- 1 ½ teaspns vanilla extract
- 1 can (8 oz) crushed undrained pineapple
- 2 cupsfuls of mashed ripe bananas
- 1 cupsful of minced pecans

For the cream cheese frosting:

- 1 package (8 oz) softened cream cheese
- ½ cupsful softened untable-salted butter
- 4 cupsfuls of groundeded sugar
- 2 teaspns vanilla extract
- Minced pecans for garnish

Cooking Instructions:

- Begin by foreheating your oven to 350°F (175°C). Prepare three 9-inch cake pans by greasing and flouring them, and lining the bottoms with parchment paper.
- In a container, whisk together flour, sugar, baking soda, table-salt, and cinnamon till well combined.
- Add beaten eggs, vegetable oil, and vanilla extract to the dry ingredients, and mix till the batter is smooth and well incorporated.

- Fold in crushed pineapple, mashed bananas, and minced pecans into the batter.

- Divide the batter evenly among the prepared cake pans and bake for roughly 25-30 mins, or till the cakes are fully cooked.

- While the cakes are baking, prepare the cream cheese frosting by beating together cream cheese and butter till smooth. Gradually add groundeded sugar and vanilla extract, and continue to beat till the frosting is smooth and creamy.

- Once the cakes have cooled, assemble the layers by placing one cake layer on a stand or serving platter, and spreading a layer of frosting on top. Repeat the process with the remaining two layers, and then frost the sides of the cake as well.

- Garnish the top of the cake with minced pecans, and refrigerate for at least an hour prior serving to allow the frosting to set.

Texas Sheet Cakes

Sheet Cake is a classic dessert that originated in the Lone Star State. It's a moist and decadent chocolate cake that's topped with a rich and creamy frosting.

Prep Time: 20 mins

Cooking Duration: 25 mins

Equipment:

- A large container
- A medium saucepan
- A 15x10x1 inch baking pan
- A whisk or electric mixer
- Measuring cupsfuls and spoons
- Spatula
- Oven

Ingredients:

For cake:

- 2 cupsfuls of all-purpose flour
- 2 cupsfuls of granulated sugar
- 1 teaspn baking soda
- Half teaspn table-salt
- 1 cupsful of untable-salted butter
- Qtr. cupsful of cocoa grounded
- 1 cupsful of water
- Half cupsful of buttermilk
- 2 large beaten eggs
- 1 teaspn vanilla extract

For frosting:

- Half cupsful of untable-salted butter
- Qtr. cupsful of cocoa grounded
- 6 tabspns milk
- 1 teaspn vanilla extract
- 3 Half cupsfuls of groundeded sugar

Cooking Instructions:

- Prewarm your oven reaching 350°F (175°C).
- Begin by combining the flour, sugar, baking soda, and table-salt in a large container. Whisk till well combined. In a separate saucepan, melt the butter.
- Add cocoa grounded and water, stirring till smooth. Bring the mixture to a boil, then Withdraw from heat.
- Pour the chocolate mixture into the dry ingredients and stir till combined. Next, add buttermilk, beaten eggs, and vanilla extract to the mixture, and stir till well combined.

- Pour the batter into a 15x10x1 inch greased baking pan, using a spatula to smooth the top. Bake for 20-25 mins, or till a toothpick inserted into the center of the cake comes out clean.
- While the cake is baking, prepare the frosting. In a saucepan, melt the butter. Add cocoa grounded and milk, stirring till smooth.
- Bring the mixture to a boil, then Withdraw from heat. Stir in the vanilla extract and groundeded sugar till well combined.
- Once the cake is done, let it cool for 5 mins prior pouring the warm frosting over the top.
- Use a spatula to spread the frosting evenly over the cake.
- Allow the cake to cool completely prior serving.
- Slice and enjoy your delicious Texas sheet cake.

Sopaipillas

Sopaipillas are a popular delicious and crispy fried pastry in Texas. They are usually served as a dessert or a snack, and are often accompanied by honey or cinnamon sugar.

Prep Time: 1 hr 15 mins

Cooking Duration: 30 mins

Equipment:

- Large container
- Rolling pin
- Cutting board
- Deep frying pan
- Slotted spoon
- Paper towels

Ingredients:

- 2 cupsfuls of all-purpose flour
- 1 tabspn baking grounded
- ½ teaspn table-salt
- 3 tabspns vegetable shortening
- 2/3 cupsful of warm water
- Vegetable oil for frying
- Honey or cinnamon sugar for serving

Cooking Instructions:

- To make sopaipillas, begin by whisking together flour, baking grounded, and table-salt in a container.
- Add vegetable shortening and mix with a fork till the mixture is crumbly.
- Gradually pour in warm water while continuing to mix with a fork till a ball of dough forms.
- Transfer the dough to a floured surface and knead for around 2 mins, till it becomes smooth and elastic.
- Cover the dough with a damp cloth and cool for 30 mins.
- Next, heat 2 inches of vegetable oil in a deep fry-pan over medium-high heat till it reaches 375° F.
- On a floured surface, roll out the dough to a thickness of around ¼ inch, then cut it into squares or triangles of your wanted size.
- Carefully drop a few pieces of dough into the hot oil, being careful not to overcrowd the pan. Fry each piece for 2-3 mins, or till they puff up and turn golden brown.
- Use a slotted spoon to withdraw the sopaipillas from the oil and Position them on paper towels to drain any excess oil.
- Finally, serve the sopaipillas while they're still warm, either drizzled with honey or sprinkled with cinnamon sugar.

German Chocolate Cake

German Chocolate Cake is a rich and indulgent cake that features layers of moist chocolate cake filled with a sweet and creamy coconut pecan frosting.

Prep Time: 30 mins

Cooking Duration: 30-35 mins

Equipment:

- 3 (9-inch) round cake pans
- Containers
- Hand mixer or stand mixer
- Saucepan
- Whisk
- Spatula
- Parchment paper

Ingredients:

For the Cake:

- 2 cupsfuls of all-purpose flour
- 2 cupsfuls of granulated sugar
- ¾ cupsful of unsweetened cocoa grounded
- 2 teaspn baking grounded
- 1 ½ teaspn baking soda
- 1 teaspn table-salt
- 1 cupsful of buttermilk
- ½ cupsful vegetable oil
- 2 large eggs
- 2 teaspns vanilla extract
- 1 cupsful of hot coffee

For the Frosting:

- 1 cupsful of evaporated milk
- 1 cupsful of granulated sugar
- 3 large egg yolks
- ½ cupsful of untable-salted butter
- 1 teaspn vanilla extract
- 1 ½ cupsfuls sweetened coconut shreds
- 1 cupsful of minced pecans

Cooking Instructions:

- Foreheat your oven to 350°F and grease three 9-inch round cake pans. Line them with parchment paper.
- In a large container, mix together flour, sugar, cocoa grounded, baking grounded, baking soda, and table-salt using a whisk.
- Add the wet ingredients to the dry ingredients and mix till well combined.

- Pour in hot coffee and stir till smooth.

- Divide the batter equally between the three cake pans.

- Bake in the foreheated oven for 30-35 mins or till a toothpick inserted in the center comes out clean.

- To make the frosting, combine evaporated milk, sugar, egg yolks, butter, and vanilla extract in a saucepan. Cook over medium heat, stirring constantly, till the mixture thickens and turns golden brown.

- Withdraw the frosting from the heat and stir in coconut and minced pecans.

- Allow the frosting to cool for 15-20 mins or till it thickens to a spreading consistency.

- To assemble the cake, Position one cake layer on a cake stand or serving plate. Spread a generous amount of frosting over the top of the cake. Repeat with the remaining two cake layers, spreading frosting between each layer and on top of the cake.

Frozen Bananas

Frozen Bananas are a fun and healthy snack that is perfect for hot summer days. This recipe features ripe bananas coated in a creamy peanut butter mixture, then frozen till they're firm and slightly crunchy on the outside.

Prep Time: 15 mins

Freezing Time: 2-3 hrs

Equipment:

- Parchment paper
- Baking sheet
- Small container
- Whisk
- Spoon
- Knife
- Cutting board

Ingredients:

- 4 ripe bananas
- ½ cupsful of creamy peanut butter
- ¼ cupsful honey
- 1 teaspn vanilla extract
- Table-salt
- 1 cupsful peanuts, minced (optional)

Cooking Instructions:

- Prepare a baking sheet by lining it with parchment paper and set it aside.
- In a small container, combine the peanut butter, honey, vanilla extract, and table-salt till you have a smooth mixture.
- Cut the bananas in half crosswise, peel them, and then insert a popsicle stick into the cut end of each half.
- Dip each banana half into the peanut butter mixture, making sure to spread the mixture evenly over the banana using a spoon.
- If wanted, roll the coated bananas in minced peanuts, pressing lightly to help the peanuts adhere to the peanut butter mixture.
- Arrange the coated bananas on the prepared baking sheet and freeze them for 2-3 hrs till they are firm.
- After freezing, take the bananas out of the baking sheet and store them in an airtight container in the freezer.
- Serve your delicious Texas Frozen Bananas straight from the freezer.

Cinnamon Rolls

Cinnamon Rolls are a sweet and indulgent treat perfect for breakfast, brunch or any special occasion. They are fluffy, buttery, and loaded with cinnamon sugar filling, and topped with a rich cream cheese glaze.

Prep Time: 2 hrs 30 mins

Cooking Duration: 25 mins

Equipment:

- Stand mixer or large container
- Rolling pin
- 9x13 inch baking dish
- Pastry brush
- Sharp knife
- Container for glaze

List of ingredients:

For the dough:

- 1 cupsful whole milk
- 2 ¼ teaspn active dry yeast
- ½ cupsful granulated sugar
- 1/3 cupsful untable-salted butter, melted
- 2 large eggs
- 1 teaspn table-salt
- 4 ½ cupsfuls of all-purpose flour

For the filling:

- ½ cupsful of untable-salted butter, softened
- 1 cupsful of light brown sugar
- 2 tabspns ground cinnamon

For glaze:

- 4 oz softened cream cheese
- ¼ cupsful softened untable-salted butter
- 1 ½ cupsfuls groundeded sugar
- ½ teaspn vanilla extract
- 1-2 tabspn whole milk

Cooking Instructions:

- In a saucepan, warm up milk over low heat till it reaches 110°F (43°C). Withdraw from heat and sprinkle yeast on top. Let it sit for no less than 5 mins till the yeast is foamy.
- In a separate container, combine sugar, melted butter, eggs, and table-salt. Add milk and yeast mixture and stir to combine.
- Gradually add flour to the mixture, and use a stand mixer or mix by hand till dough is smooth and elastic. Use a dough hook attachment and knead the dough around 5 mins on medium speed if using a stand mixer.

- Cover the container with a kitchen towel and let dough rise in a warm Position around 1 hour or till it has doubled in size.

- Foreheat oven to 350° F (175° C).

- In a container, combine softened butter, brown sugar, and cinnamon to make the filling.

- Once the dough has risen, move it to a floured surface and roll it out into a large rectangle, about ¼ inch thick.

- Use a pastry brush to spread the filling mixture evenly over the surface of the dough.

- Starting from the long edge, tightly roll the dough up towards the other end. Cut the rolled dough into 12-15 slices using a sharp knife.

- Position the rolls in a greased 9x13 inch baking dish and let them rise again around 30 mins.

- Bake the rolls in the foreheated oven around 20-25 mins or till golden brown and cooked through.

- While the rolls are baking, prepare the cream cheese glaze. In a container, mix softened cream cheese, butter, groundeded sugar, vanilla extract, and enough milk to create a smooth and creamy consistency.

- Once the rolls are done, withdraw them from the oven and let them cool for a few mins. Drizzle the cream cheese glaze over the top of the rolls and serve them warm.

Cowboy Cookies

Cowboy Cookies are a hearty, sweet treat that combines the flavors of chocolate, coconut, and pecans in a chewy oatmeal cookie.

Prep Time: 15 mins

Cooking Duration: 12-15 mins

Equipment:

- Oven
- Baking sheet
- Container
- Whisk or fork
- Measuring cupsfuls and spoons
- Rubber spatula
- Cooling rack

Ingredients:

- 1 cupsful all-purpose flour
- 1 teaspn baking grounded
- 1 teaspn baking soda
- ½ teaspn table-salt
- 1 cupsful untable-salted butter, at room temperature
- 1 cupsful granulated sugar
- 1 cupsful brown sugar, packed
- 2 large eggs
- 1 teaspn vanilla extract
- 2 cupsfuls old-fashioned oats
- 1 cupsful semi-sweet chocolate chips
- 1 cupsful shredded coconut
- 1 cupsful minced pecans

Cooking Instructions:

- Prewarm your oven reaching 350°F (180°C) and line a baking sheet with parchment paper.
- In a container, combine the flour, baking grounded, baking soda, and table-salt. Set aside.
- In a large container, cream together the butter, brown and granulated sugar till light and fluffy.
- Add the eggs and vanilla extract to the butter mixture and mix till well combined.
- Gradually add the flour mixture to the butter mixture and mix till just combined.
- Add the oats, chocolate chips, shredded coconut, and minced pecans to the dough and mix till evenly distributed.
- Use a cookie scoop to drop dough balls onto the prepared baking sheet, leaving about 2 inches between each cookie.
- Bake the cookies for 12-15 mins.
- Serve and enjoy your delicious Texas Cowboy Cookies!

Banana Pudding

Banana Pudding is a delightful and creamy dessert that combines layers of vanilla pudding, sliced bananas, and vanilla wafers. The dessert is then topped off with whipped cream, creating a delicious and refreshing treat that everyone will love.

Prep Time: 30 mins

Cooking Duration: 10-15 mins

Equipment:

- Medium-sized container
- Whisk
- Large container
- 9x13 inch baking dish
- Saucepan
- Mixing spoon

Ingredients:

- 1 box of vanilla wafers (12 oz.)
- 1 package of instant vanilla pudding mix (5.1 oz.)
- 4 medium-sized ripe bananas, sliced
- 2 cupsfuls of cold milk
- 1 teaspn of vanilla extract
- 1 cupsful of heavy whipping cream
- 1 can of condensed milk (14 oz.)
- 2 tabspns of groundeded sugar

Cooking Instructions:

- Foreheat your oven to 350° F and prepare a baking dish.
- In a container, whisk together instant vanilla pudding mix, 2 cupsfuls of cold milk, condensed milk, and vanilla extract till smooth.
- Create a layer of vanilla wafers at the bottom of the baking dish, followed by a layer of sliced bananas.
- Spread half of the pudding mixture on top of the bananas and vanilla wafers, ensuring it covers the entire dish.
- Repeat the process with another layer of vanilla wafers, sliced bananas, and the remaining pudding mixture.
- Bake the pudding in the foreheated oven for 10-15 mins or till the top is set.
- Withdraw the pudding from the oven and let it cool completely.
- In another container, whisk heavy whipping cream and groundeded sugar together till stiff peaks form.
- Spread the whipped cream evenly over the cooled pudding.
- Add another layer of vanilla wafers and sliced bananas on top of the whipped cream.
- Refrigerate the pudding for at least 2 hrs prior serving.

Texas Carrot Cakes

Texas Carrot Cake is a classic southern-style dessert that's moist, tender, and packed with warm spices and juicy carrots. The cream cheese frosting on the top adds a delicious zesty sweetness that complements the cake perfectly.

Prep Time: 20 mins

Cooking Duration: 40-45 mins

Equipment:

- Large container
- Hand mixer or stand mixer
- Measuring cupsfuls and spoons
- Mixing spatula
- 9-inch cake pan
- Parchment paper
- Cooling rack

Ingredients:

For cake:

- 2 cupsfuls of all-purpose flour
- 2 teaspns baking grounded
- 1 teaspn baking soda
- 1 teaspn cinnamon
- ½ teaspn nutmeg
- ½ teaspn table-salt
- 3 large eggs at room temperature
- 1 ½ cupsfuls of granulated sugar
- 1 cupsful of vegetable oil
- 2 teaspns vanilla extract
- 2 cupsfuls of grated carrots

For frosting:

- 8-ounce cream cheese at room temperature
- ½ cupsful of untable-salted butter at room temperature
- 4 cupsfuls of groundeded sugar
- 2 teaspns vanilla extract

Cooking Instructions:

- Begin by foreheating your oven to 350° F and greasing a 9-inch cake pan with cooking spray or butter. Line the bottom of the pan with parchment paper.
- In a large container, combine the flour, baking grounded, baking soda, cinnamon, nutmeg, and table-salt. Whisk well to combine.
- In another container, beat the eggs, sugar, oil, and vanilla extract together till smooth.
- Add the dry ingredients to the wet mixture and mix till well combined.
- Fold in the grated carrots till evenly distributed in the batter.

- Pour the batter into the prepared cake pan and use a spatula to smooth out the top.
- Bake the cake for 40-45 mins or till a toothpick inserted into the center of the cake comes out clean.
- Withdraw the cake from the oven and let it cool in the pan around 10 mins. Carefully withdraw the cake from the pan and Position it on a cooling rack to cool completely.
- While the cake is cooling, prepare the frosting. In a large container, beat the cream cheese and butter till smooth.
- Gradually add in the groundeded sugar and vanilla extract and continue to beat till the frosting is light and fluffy.
- Once the cake is cooled, spread the frosting evenly over the top and sides of the cake.
- Serve the cake immediately or store it in an airtight container in the ice-box for up to 3 days.

Texas-Style Donuts

Texas donuts are big, fluffy, delicious, and satisfying.

Prep Time: 20 mins

Cooking Duration: 15-20 mins

Equipment:

- Large container
- Whisk or electric mixer
- Rolling pin
- Donut cutter or biscuit cutter
- Deep fryer or large pan
- Spider or slotted spoon
- Paper towels
- Small saucepan

Ingredients:

For dough:

- 4 cupsfuls of all-purpose flour
- 1/3 cupsful of granulated sugar
- 1 teaspn table-salt
- 2 tabspns active dry yeast
- 1 cupsful warm milk
- 4 large eggs
- ½ cupsful untable-salted butter, softened

For the glaze:

- 2 cupsfuls of groundeded sugar
- ¼ cupsful of milk
- 1 teaspn of vanilla extract

Cooking Instructions:

- Mix together flour, sugar, table-salt, and active dry yeast in a container.
- In a separate container, whisk warm milk, eggs, and softened butter till smooth.
- Add milk mixture to flour mixture and stir till dough forms.
- Knead the dough till it's smooth and elastic, about 5-7 mins.
- Put the dough in a container and cover with a clean cloth. Let it rise in a warm Position till it doubles in size, about 1 hour.
- Once risen, punch down the dough and roll it out on a floured surface till it's ½ inch thick.
- Utilize a donut cutter or biscuit cutter to cut out the donuts and donut holes.
- Heat oil in a deep fryer or large pan till it reaches 375° F.
- Gently lower the donuts and donut holes into the hot oil using a spider or slotted spoon. Fry till golden brown, flipping once, about 2-3 mins per side.

- Withdraw the donuts from the oil and Position them on paper towels to drain any excess oil.

- Warm milk in a small saucepan over low heat. Add groundeded sugar and vanilla extract and whisk till smooth.

- Dip each donut in the glaze, turning to coat both sides.

- Position the glazed donuts on a wire rack to cool and allow the glaze to set.

Apple Pie

Apple pie has a buttery crumb topping added to give it a crunchy and sweet finish. With the combination of sweet and tart apples, warm spices, and crumbly topping, it's sure to please your guests.

Prep Time: 30 mins

Cooking Duration: 50-60 mins

Equipment:

- 9-inch pie dish
- Containers
- Cutting board
- Knife
- Measuring cupsfuls and spoons
- Pastry blender or fork
- Aluminum foil

Ingredients:

For Crust:

- 1¼ cupsfuls of all-purpose flour
- ¼ teaspn table-salt
- ½ cupsful untable-salted butter, cold and cubed
- 3-4 tabspns ice water

For Filling:

- 6 cupsfuls peeled and sliced apples (a mix of sweet and tart apples)
- ¼ cupsful of all-purpose flour
- ½ cupsful of granulated sugar
- ¼ cupsful of brown sugar
- 1 teaspn ground cinnamon
- ½ teaspn ground nutmeg
- ¼ teaspn table-salt
- 2 tabspns untable-salted butter, melted
- 1 tabspn lemon juice

For Crumb Topping:

- 1 cupsful of all-purpose flour
- ½ cupsful of granulated sugar
- ½ cupsful of untable-salted butter, melted
- 1 teaspn ground cinnamon

Cooking Instructions:

- Foreheat the reaching 375°F (190°C).

- Mix together flour and table-salt in a container to make the crust. Add cubed butter and use a fork to cut it into the flour till it resembles coarse sand.

- Mix in ice water till the dough comes together. Form it into a ball, flatten it into a disc, and wrap it in plastic wrap. Refrigerate for at least 30 mins.

- In a large container, combine sliced apples, flour, granulated sugar, brown sugar, cinnamon, nutmeg, table-salt, melted butter, and lemon juice to prepare the filling. Stir till the apples are coated.

- In a separate container, combine flour, granulated sugar, melted butter, and cinnamon to prepare the crumb topping. Stir till the mixture forms large crumbs.

- Roll out the chilled pie crust on a floured surface and fit it into a 9-inch pie dish. Trim the edges and crimp as wanted.

- Pour the apple filling inside the pie crust, spreading it out evenly.

- Sprinkle the crumb topping, covering it completely.

- To prevent the edges of the pie from browning too quickly, cover them with foil.

- Bake the pie for 50-60 mins.

- Once the pie is done, withdraw it from the oven and allow it to cool on a wire rack for at least 30 mins prior slicing and serving.

- Serve with a dollop of whipped cream or a scoop of vanilla ice cream, if wanted.

Conclusion

As I sit here reflecting on my memories of growing up in Texas, I can't help but feel a sense of nostalgia. Even though I've since moved away from the Lone Star State, Texas will always hold a unique Position in my heart.

One of the things that I miss most about Texas is the food. There's just something about the way that Texans cook that can't be replicated anywhere else. Whether it's the smoky flavor of a perfectly cooked brisket or the spice of a plate of chicken fried steak, Texas cuisine is truly one-of-a-kind.

But Texas culture is about more than just food. It's about a way of life, a sense of community, and a pride in where you come from. I'll never forget the way that my neighbors banded together after Hurricane Harvey to help each other rebuild their homes and their lives. It was a testament to the resilience and strength of the people of Texas.

And even though I've been away from Texas for some Time now, I still carry the lessons that I learned growing up there with me every day. I've learned the value of hard work, the importance of family and community, and the need to take care of each other.

So, as I look back on my memories of Texas, I'm filled with a sense of gratitude for all of the experiences that I've had there. From my grandmother's homemade chili to the rodeos and BBQ competitions, Texas has given me so much.

And even though I may be living in a different state now, I still consider myself a Texan at heart. Because being a Texan isn't just about where you live or what you eat, it's about the spirit and the values that you carry with you no matter where you go.

So, here's to Texas, the Position that will always be a part of me. Whether I'm sitting down to a plate of tacos or reminiscing about my childhood memories, Texas will always hold a special Position in my heart. And I know that no matter where life takes me, I'll always be proud to be a Texan.

Made in the USA
Columbia, SC
25 June 2023

19224278R00076